Selfish Little Cow

JENNY HARDING
with MARIA MALONE

First published 2015
ISBN: 978-1515118206

Cover design: Emma King at The Curved House
Formatting: Polgarus Studio

For my children, Michele and Michael, who now seem to think they're my parents …

Prologue

I killed my parents.

They were on the road when they died, driving to London, when they should have been at the seaside taking things easy. It was me they were coming to see. Me they cut short their holiday for. Mum and Dad, tootling along, minding their own business, Mum at the wheel, when some young lad in a white van came flying up behind. The impact flipped their car into the air, turned it over and dumped it on its roof where it burst into flames.

It was June, 1969, a few days before my seventeenth birthday.

That week, they had wanted me to go with them to the caravan at Canvey Island but I had other plans. Stuff I didn't want them to know about. There'd have been ructions if they knew I was meeting my ex, Nick Benson. His name was mud in our house, and with good reason. All the time he was seeing me, saying he wanted to marry me, he had another girl on the go. I so loved him and he broke my heart, left me in pieces. It was Mum who put me back together. After what he'd done, she didn't want him anywhere near me.

Trouble was, he wouldn't let go. Wherever I went he was there – hanging about on the edge of the dance floor, parked up outside the garage where I worked, engine running. In the end, I agreed to see him. On the quiet.

If only Mum hadn't phoned home it would have been all right. *If only*. My sister, Patricia, couldn't wait to tell her I'd been out with Nick, little cow that I was. Mum went mad, wanting to know what I thought I was playing at, but I wouldn't get on the phone and tell her. I was too scared. Patricia called me all the names, waved the phone in my face, while I sat there, mouth shut, stubborn, thinking she could turn the air blue for all I cared, I wasn't about to speak to Mum and get it in the neck.

I knew what she would say, anyway.

Miles away, in the caravan, thinking the worst, Mum was worried sick. That was it. Holiday over. The next day, they packed up early and headed home.

When I think about it now, all I had to do was speak to her and say she didn't have to worry because I wasn't getting back with him. I really wasn't. A few words, that was all, and I could have put her mind at rest.

I wish I had.

I never thought I wouldn't get another chance.

1.

If I close my eyes it's as if I'm there, on the scullery step, my mother at the sink, cold water gushing from the single tap jutting from the wall. She fills a bucket and heaves it to a giant cauldron, an ugly old thing she calls a copper, in the corner of the room, moves about the scullery, filling the copper, lighting the gas underneath, heating the water. Wash day. This is how the laundry gets done. Her hands are raw from being in and out of water and when she lifts the lid of the copper steam rises and makes her face pink. She wipes a hand on her apron and pushes a dark damp curl off her forehead. The chill from the stone step I'm sitting on makes me shiver. I hug my knees to my chest and wait, watching her work. It looks back-breaking, the fetching and carrying, but in a house with no hot water it is how things are done. She turns and gives me a smile. My mother has the brightest eyes. Blue-grey. With the last of the clothes in the copper, she pours tea from the pot that always seems to be on the go, and we take it into the living room where there's a fire blazing. Mum hoists me onto the table and

3

flops into the dining chair facing me. She lets out a sigh and says something about her bones being weary, making a joke of it. She never, ever complains, my mum. My legs dangle over the end of the table and brush against her knee. She tips tea from the cup into the saucer and tells me to let it cool a bit before having a drink. Blows on hers, takes a sip. I do the same. I can't remember when I started drinking tea. As far as I know, I always have. We sit there, me on the table, Mum on the dining chair, the only one we've got, feeling the heat from the fire. At four years old, I am too young to think about anything much although, now, looking back, one thing I was certain of was that I was happy. Those innocent times when I was too little to have started school, when it was Mum and me at home together and no one else around, I was in my element. It might have been the happiest I ever was.

I thought that was how it would be forever.

My mother didn't want me.

She was forty-five when she found out she was expecting again and by then had six children already – a boy and five girls. The youngest, my sister Patricia, was a toddler, about two, and there was my poor mum, another one on the way. Not what she or my dad had planned. It must have seemed the cruellest of blows. As far as they were concerned, they had all the children they wanted. They might even have dared entertain ideas of life getting that bit easier as the older ones began leaving home. My eldest sister, Jean, twenty-something by then, had already moved out although, even with her gone, conditions were cramped.

Home was a terraced property, a funny old three-storey place, in Hamilton Road, Walthamstow, in London, sandwiched in between a sweet shop and a grocer's. My parents, Alfred and Elsie Jones, rented it. At some point, long before they moved in, the front part of the property had been a shop that over time had become disused and ended up a dirty hovel full of rubbish and old inner tubes, the big ones you got on lorries. The window that faced onto the street didn't even have glass in it, so the place had a sorry-looking, rundown air. You went through the old shop front to get to the living room, the one room with a fire, which was the only heating in the whole place. Off the living room, the scullery was down a flight of steps. The toilet was out the back in a rickety wooden outhouse full of creepy-crawlies. Upstairs, Mum and Dad's bedroom was on the first floor. Up another flight at the top of the house, my sisters, Lizzie, Christine, Gillian, and Patricia squashed in together. Alf, my brother, who everyone called Boy, was in the room next door. Come to think of it, he did all right, the only one with his own bedroom.

For my mum, putting food on the table meant being creative with what little housekeeping money there was; making do, eking things out. Things were tight. If the rent was due and she didn't have it she wouldn't answer the door to the rent man. It's no wonder an unplanned pregnancy in her mid-forties was devastating. Another baby held no joy for her, only fear at the prospect of an extra mouth to feed in a house where there wasn't always enough to go round as it was. She didn't see how it could be done. Upstairs on her own in her freezing bedroom, thinking things through in peace while the others clustered around the fire in the living room, she must have felt desperate. Enough to throw herself down the stairs; not just once, a few times. It made no difference. The child she felt sure she could not afford to have was tough, a survivor.

It – *I* – clung to life.

She had me at home in the big bedroom on the top floor, the one my sisters shared, and named me Jennifer after a friend she'd had in her teens. I was always Jenny.

How Mum felt when she was expecting me seemed to be forgotten once I was born and I never had any sense of being unwanted. The two of us were close as anything. It was only as I got older I heard the stories about what had gone on when she was expecting me. She never told me, never said a word. It was something my sisters took pleasure in; how they'd be downstairs, Dad in his usual armchair at the side of the fire, Mum upstairs, and out of nowhere there'd be a series of thumps and bumps and an almighty crash at the foot of the stairs. In the living room, they'd look at each other and someone would say, 'There's Mum throwing herself down the stairs again.'

The first time I heard about this, it didn't mean much. Too young to understand, I suppose. Later, when it sank on what my mother had done – and why – all I could think was that she must have been in a dreadful state.

Out of her mind with worry.

Now, when I picture her in a heap at the foot of the stairs, no one going to see if she was all right, I struggle to take it in. I keep thinking there had to be a first time, before it became something everyone shrugged at, when they must have gone running. You'd think so, anyway. I wonder how many times she fell before no one took any notice any more and left her to pick herself up. I often think about her joining the others in the living room, chasing one of my sisters from her armchair at the side of the fire, and no one saying a word.

2.

I climbed up the stack of mucky old inner tubes and dropped down inside. The shop bit at the front of the house with its mess and jumble made a good den. In the dark, out of sight, I made believe I had crawled through a narrow tunnel into a secret chamber. A witch's lair. I shivered, thinking about ghosts hidden in the shadows, and shouted to my friend Catherine to get a move on. She landed with a thud beside me and we sat on the damp floor, knees almost touching, giggling, nervous.

'It's haunted in here,' I said, a bit braver now I wasn't on my own.

Catherine didn't answer, just struck a match and lit the candle she had brought, holding it in front of her face.

'You go first,' she said.

In the light from the candle, she had a strange, shadowy look.

'Don't hold it like that,' I said, not liking what the flickering flame was doing to her eyes, making them hooded and mean-looking.

'Why, you scared?'

'Course not,' I lied. 'You're getting wax on me, that's all.'

She dripped wax onto the floor and stood the candle up in it. Her face went back to being normal. She dug a small paper bag out of the pocket of her dress and between us we polished off the rest of the dolly mixtures. Catherine's dad had the sweet shop next door so she always had a bag of something or other.

I began to tell her about a girl who was sent away to a big old house in the middle of nowhere and never saw her family for years. The people she went to live with were strict and when she got into trouble they put her in a cottage on her own and locked her in. It was haunted, the cottage, by the man who used to live there and had been found hanging from the banister. While the girl polished and cleaned, the ghost of the man watched, waiting for a chance to grab her. Even though she never saw him she knew he was there.

'She could feel him,' I said. 'The air went cold, even when it was a hot day. That's how she knew.'

A chill went through me and I shifted position, trying to find somewhere to put my bare feet other than the concrete floor. Catherine gave me a nudge, wanting me to get on with the story.

'There was a secret panel in the big house,' I said. 'And a passage that went all the way to the cottage. That's how the ghost never got her.'

Catherine listened, wide-eyed, thrilled.

'I don't believe you,' she said, eventually.

I shrugged, picked at a scab on my knee. 'Don't care.'

The story about the haunted cottage came from my mother. I knew from being very small that Mum's childhood had been terrible rough. Her family had come from Ireland before the Great War with very little. Mum had an accent that made her stand out and went to school dirty, her shoes tied on with string. She was always getting picked on. When she was about six years old a policeman saw how neglected-looking she was and took her home. She got a slap from my nan for bringing the police to the door, and ended up in a children's home. When they bathed her and washed her hair they discovered a beautiful child underneath the layers of filth.

She loved to tell me about the children's home, the haunted cottage with its secret passage, and how she would sneak along it to get to Jennifer, her best friend.

Mum was sixteen when she left the home. Not long after she was hit by a lorry and awarded compensation, which my nan took off her. I'm making Nan sound like an awful woman but she had seven children, so life can't have been easy. I understand now why she was the way she was.

I didn't see much of my nan but I always found her scary. On the few occasions I went to visit I hid behind my mother's skirt. Nan was a fierce woman with long grey hair, plaited and coiled around her head, deep set blue eyes and a hump on her back. It was the hump that disturbed me. I was convinced she was a witch. Then again, I was the seventh child of a seventh child so the chances were she thought the same about me.

Jean, Alf, Lizzie, Christine, Gillian, Patricia, me. That was the order. Jean, the eldest, was married by the time I was born and

I never really knew her. Mostly, it was Gillian and Patricia I spent my time with. Ours was the family other kids weren't allowed to play with. Thinking back, we were a bit wild-looking. I had masses of curly fair hair down my back and tore around the streets barefoot most of the time. The soles of my feet were black, like leather. One night I stayed at Jean's house and shared a bed with my cousin, him at one end, me at the other, and I remember shouting out, 'Jimmy's got pink feet!' Until then, I thought everyone's feet were black, like mine. I was always covered in cuts and bruises and scabs from some scrape or other. It wasn't that we were bad, no worse than any other kids in Hamilton Road, anyway, but the neighbours still preferred us to stick to our end of the street. If we strayed too far and ended up in Oakfield Road, where they thought they were a cut above, they'd be banging on the windows chasing us away.

'Go down your own end, you!'

The Peter French shirt factory was not far from where we lived and I'd go up there with Gillian and Patricia and climb over a wall to get in. What we were after were the cardboard rolls the shirt material came on. We'd use them as weapons and whack each other round the head. It was great fun until the watchman came along and we had to make a run for it. Me and Gillian would dive under the gate and get away but Patricia was too fat and got stuck. She was always getting caught. Every time she got a telling-off she seemed to think it was my fault and complained to Mum.

When we weren't at the shirt factory, we'd go to the washing machine shop a few streets away and ask for one of their big cardboard boxes, drag it home, and make a doll's house. We'd get a blanket from Mum for the carpet and cut out squares for windows. It would keep us occupied for hours. Not every game needed cardboard. For magic grottos we'd raid someone's garden and help ourselves to soil, shape it into a cross and decorate it with flowers – ones that had probably come from the same garden as the soil. We'd sit in the street at the front of the house and ask everyone who went past for a penny for the grotto. Once we'd made enough money we'd go to the sweet shop next door for two ounces of aniseed balls or fruit salad chews that were a penny for four.

Once a week was bath night. The old tin tub that hung on the wall outside would be brought into the scullery and filled and we'd take it in turns and share the water. Because I was the youngest, I went first, but if I'd fallen out with one of my sisters I'd ask to go in just before her and pee in the water. It was my way of getting my own back. I never got found out.

Just as well.

They'd have killed me.

3.

When I started school at the age of five I still had a dummy, a big brown one that Mum would dunk in a jar of something called Virol, for vitamins. On my first day at St Andrew's Infants, in Walthamstow, Mum got me into a navy pinafore with pleats and a sash and took me as far as the alley that led to the playground. I didn't like the idea of going down the dark little passage with its high walls so I hung back. Then Mum said she was off and I screamed and cried and begged to go with her. She wasn't having any of it and left me there, making a scene, until I gave up and went in like everybody else. I hadn't worked out that from then on I'd be going to school every day, and convinced myself that if I could only manage to stick it out, just the once, I'd be able to stay at home with Mum, like before. It was a shock when I had to put my uniform on again the next day and go off to St Andrew's with my sister, Patricia, who was in the class a couple of years above me. This time, Mum didn't come. After that first day, she never took me again.

I missed being at home with Mum but there were things I liked about school. Every morning at break we each got a bottle of milk and I looked forward to the monitors coming round with a crate of miniature bottles. School dinners I loved: meat pie, cabbage, sausages, onion gravy, scoops of mashed potato, semolina. I enjoyed it all, maybe because we didn't get that kind of food at home where the main meal was often something we called milk and buppy – warm milk with bread floating in it – probably all Mum could afford at the time. What I didn't like about school was the stale plimsoll smell that hung over everything. I missed my dummy too. Every day, as soon as I got home, I got on a chair so I could get it down from the shelf where it was kept. One day I looked for it and it wasn't there. My sister, Lizzie, said it was all maggoty and they'd had to throw it out. I didn't know what maggots were.

I hadn't been at school very long, a few weeks, when I got sick. I felt really poorly but didn't want to tell my teacher, Miss Simmonds, because if you weren't well you got sent to the hall and had to sit in a deckchair and everyone going past stared at you. Eventually, I felt so bad, dreadful sick, I had to run to the wash basins in the cloakroom. After a while, a boy from my class came out with some tissues and found me, still hanging over the sink. I couldn't stop heaving. What was making me feel worse was the overpowering smell of sweaty plimsolls. I couldn't tell you how long it was before the headmaster came to see what was going on and got a lady I didn't know, one of the cooks, I think, to take me home.

There was no answer when she knocked on our front door,

not that I expected Mum to open up in case it was the rent man. Mr and Mrs Pike, who had the grocer's shop next door, took me in and got Mum to come for me. She put me straight to bed and called Dr Frederick. Next thing, he was phoning for an ambulance and I was on my way to the Connaught Hospital, Mum in the back beside me, white-faced, telling me not to be scared, that it would all be alright. By then, I felt so rotten I was beyond caring about being rushed to hospital in an ambulance with its bells clanging.

When I got to the Connaught the nurses who assessed me wanted to know why I was covered in scabs and bruises, maybe thinking I was being knocked about at home, but I was always battered-looking from playing out. They put me in a bed in a glass cubicle at the end of the ward nearest the door. Later, someone told me the cubicle was for patients who were dangerously ill and the reason it was so close to the exit was so they could get you out with the least disruption to other patients if you didn't recover.

I was diagnosed with rheumatic fever, a heart and respiratory disease, and for the next few weeks was in and out of the glass cubicle, at times close to death. Mum and Dad came in as much as the visiting hours allowed. Even if your child was dying, you had to stick to set times. No exceptions. Visitors would gather outside the ward and the doors were kept firmly shut until Matron opened up. When visiting time was over a bell would ring and everyone had to go straight away. I was only five years old and many a time wanted my parents to stay a bit longer. It can't have been easy for them, me hanging onto them, getting upset, but they knew better than to break hospital rules. It didn't do to get on the wrong side of the matron.

What sticks in my mind about my time at the Connaught was being given drinks in a little cup with a spout and the nurses boiling up blessed needles so they could be used again and again until they were blunt and hurt like mad when you had an injection. The best thing was Mum bringing me in Corona cherryade, which I loved. I was always on at the nurses, asking when I could go home, and being told it would be the next day as long as I drank whatever horrible medicine they gave me. I believed them and did as I was told only to hear the same thing the next day … and the day after that. After three months on my best behaviour I was transferred to the heart hospital at West Wickham in Kent.

All of a sudden, I was further from home than ever.

At West Wickham they put me on a long ward in a bed that faced French windows overlooking lawns and trees in the distance. One of the first things they did when I arrived was run a bath for me. At home we had the old tin bath, nothing like the one at the hospital, which was white and gleaming and a lot bigger. Water gushed noisily from the taps and steam rose. I was used to a single cold tap over the scullery sink and, for me, the sight of water cascading into the enormous tub was terrifying. I couldn't work out what was about to happen; either they were going to put all the children into this huge bath at once or they were planning to drown me. When the nurse put me in on my own and set about bathing me, I was astonished.

There were all different ages on the ward. One girl, bigger

than me and a few years older, used to bully me and pull my plaits when the nurses weren't looking, and every day without fail a lost-looking little boy called David said his mum was coming in to see him, not that she ever did.

After being in bed for so long, I couldn't walk and had to learn all over again. The illness had left me with severe rheumatism. Every day, the nurses would take me to a room where I did exercises, building up the strength in my legs. I remember thinking I was doing really well the day I managed to pick up a pencil with my toes and everyone got excited. Once a fortnight my parents came to visit, Mum looking lovely in her best coat, a diamante brooch pinned to the collar, Dad in a grey suit and braces over his crisp white shirt, dark hair swept back and slick with Brylcreem. They always brought something for me. From being very small I liked sweets, especially chocolates, and one visit they turned up with something really special, a box of Cadbury's Vogue with a milk and plain selection. I was delighted and had them open on the bed when Matron, a stout, stern-faced woman with glasses, came sweeping down the ward. I knew I was in trouble since we were supposed to hand sweets in so everyone could share them. As she got close I shook so much the chocolates ended up on the floor, one or two rolling across the ward and ending up right in front of her. My mum got a telling off for that.

Every day, I stuck at my exercises, getting my legs to work again. It was a slow and gruelling process. I'm not sure how long it was before I could walk but I do remember being really excited when Mum and Dad turned up one weekend and I was able to take two steps on my own. After weeks of being in

bed, it felt like a huge achievement and my parents made a
fuss, hugging me and telling me how clever I was. It might
have been that visit or the one after they brought me a musical
toy and told me it had a little monkey inside playing tunes.
Once they'd gone I played with it for ages, and all I could
think about was the monkey. I must have been lonely and
desperate for a friend because I decided to set the monkey free
so he could live under my pillow and keep me company.
When one of the nurses found me with a pair of scissors
cutting open the toy and pulling it to bits she was furious.

'You wicked girl,' she said, snatching the scissors away.
'Look what you've done. You've ruined it.'

I wanted to explain, tell her about the monkey, but she was
so cross I didn't dare. She told me I was spoilt and destructive
and didn't deserve to have nice things if I was going to break
them the moment my parents turned their backs.

'You've got too much, that's your trouble,' she said, taking
the broken toy from me.

That night I lay in bed not understanding what it was I'd
done that was so bad and wondering where the little monkey
was.

As the weeks went by, I saw so little of my parents that the
nursing staff became my family. The hospital was home to me.
I didn't think much about my real home. I couldn't even
remember much about it. It got so I wasn't really sure any
more who the well-dressed couple who kept coming to see me
were or where they fitted in. I got it into my head that the
regal-looking woman at my bedside, with her shiny handbag
and gloves, a fox fur draped around her shoulders, was the

Queen Mother. The only other visitor I had was my sister, Lizzie, who came once and told me I was such a brave girl I could wear her watch. She didn't let me keep it, though.

I celebrated my sixth birthday in hospital. Mum had sent a cake iced in pink and white and decorated with flowers and a big bold number six. It was the first birthday cake I had ever seen and was completely overwhelmed. Never before had I come across anything so pretty – and it was mine. All I wanted to do was look at it. I had no idea it was something you were meant to eat. The nurses got everyone to gather round and sing happy birthday and someone told me to blow out the candles and make a wish. Then, to my horror, one of the nurses started cutting up the cake and in no time at all the best present I had ever been given was in pieces, ruined. I didn't understand about birthdays and cakes and what you did with them because it wasn't something I had experienced at home. While everyone else tucked into my cake I went back up the ward and got into bed, upset. Course, the nurses had no idea what was wrong with me. As far as they were concerned, I was horribly spoiled.

The next time my parents visited they were told what an ungrateful child I was, how I didn't want to share my birthday cake with anyone or join in, and had gone to bed in a sulk. I could see from the looks on Mum's and Dad's faces how disappointed they were. It wasn't right, though, what the nurse was saying. I wanted to say I'd loved the cake; that it was so perfect I wanted to keep it forever. If I could have done I'd have said about it being cut up and destroyed and why I got so upset, but I never got a chance – not with the nurse going on about how she despaired of me sometimes, and my parents nodding and looking so serious. In the end I said nothing.

After nine months in hospital, I was well enough to go home. The first I knew was when my parents turned up with my brother, Boy, who had brought them in the car.

'We've got a surprise for you at home,' Mum kept saying. 'Something really special.'

All I remember about the journey back to Walthamstow was crossing one of the bridges over the Thames and Mum beside me on the back seat stroking my hair and saying it wasn't much further.

The house in Hamilton Road was packed with people. My sisters, aunties, cousins, all crammed into the living room. I hadn't seen them for almost a year and had no idea who everybody was. Mum took me upstairs to the bedroom on the top floor where my other sisters slept and showed me a new single divan with a shiny red and blue eiderdown. This was the surprise she had been talking about.

'That's yours, Jenny,' she said. 'Your own bed.'

I looked at it. I didn't want my own bed. I'd had my own bed for the last twelve months, first in the Connaught and then at West Wickham. What I really wanted was to go in with my mum and dad. In the background, Lizzie peered over Mum's shoulder.

'Try it,' Mum was saying. 'Go on, it's yours.'

I told her I didn't want it.

'Well it's mine, then,' Lizzie said, delighted.

'Give her a chance,' Mum said. 'She's only just got home.'

She seemed puzzled when I said I wanted to sleep with her

and Dad.

'Don't you want your new bed? We got it for you. Go on.'

I wouldn't go near it.

Lizzie threw herself on top of the eiderdown.

'Little cow,' she said. 'That's it, I'm having it.'

Downstairs, I didn't fancy going back into the room with all those people I didn't know so I went out into the street instead. When Mum came looking for me I was sitting on a box in the middle of the road.

'Oh, if you're going to be like that you can go straight back to the hospital,' she said.

I didn't answer, didn't dare say that going back to the hospital was what I wanted most in the world. Now, when I look back, during my time at West Wickham I had become totally institutionalized. The nursing staff, the hospital regime, and the other patients were what I knew, while my family had become a distant memory.

I had to start all over again getting to know them.

4.

When I came out of the heart hospital, Mum and Dad wanted to send me to something called an open-air school. I wasn't sure what that meant. From what I could gather, it was in the countryside and when the weather was nice you had your lessons outside. It meant a coach ride every day there and back, which I didn't fancy. Some of the other children had disabilities and, if I'm honest, they scared me. I pleaded with my parents to let me go back to St Andrew's and they gave in.

Even though I'd missed a lot of school I was a quick learner and did well in my lessons. As I got older, I had lovely handwriting, and when it came to copperplate I was one of the best in the school. Our school was always winning prizes.

In those days it was normal for teachers to dish out corporal punishment, and some were brutal with it. I remember getting the ruler across my knuckles if my copperplate was anything less than perfect. I was able to write with both hands and would use whichever one wasn't tired but I got smacked for it. To make sure I wrote with my right hand the left one was tied behind my back. I was always being hit, it seemed to me. Then again, so was everybody else. If a teacher was walking up and down the aisles of the classroom every single pupil was tensed up, waiting for a slap on the head. Just for sitting next to someone who was talking or daydreaming you could end up getting a clout, and I'm not talking about a little tap; your head would really buzz. Some of the teachers had a reputation for being vicious. There was one who prowled about during morning assembly looking for kids to punish. He dragged me out by my ear one day and gave me a thump, supposedly because I wasn't singing. I was, as it happened, but you wouldn't dare argue with a teacher. One day the headmaster came into our class and called me out to the front and I wouldn't go because the week before I'd been told to go to the front and got smacked for nothing. I'd learned my lesson and refused to budge, even for the Head. It turned out I'd won a painting competition and he wanted to give me my prize, a huge selection box filled with bars of Fry's chocolate. In the end, he had to leave it under my desk.

There were things I liked about school, though. Before home time, the teacher would read us a story, which was how I discovered Enid Blyton. I could lose myself in the *Famous Five* stories. When I got a bit older I saved my pennies and went down Walthamstow market and bought the books for myself. About the closest I ever got to *Famous Five* adventures was going on field study days to Epping Forest. Our teacher, Mr Speakman, was lovely. He'd point out plants and trees and get us listening to the birdsong. We got to wear trousers and boots and take a packed lunch and be out of the classroom for a whole day.

I lived for those trips.

I always had a good imagination. On a rainy day if I couldn't play out I'd creep up to my parents' bedroom and peer through the gap in the floorboards, convinced there was treasure down there. Mum said she hadn't the faintest idea where I'd got that from and told me to come away whenever she found me flat out on the hard lino.

'You'll get cold in that eye, Jenny,' she said.

I didn't mind about my eye, not if I could find the treasure. I'd get my hand through the gap, being careful for splinters, and poke about but I never did find anything. In the end, I'd give up and go downstairs where it was warm. Mum would put coal on the fire and prod at it with the poker making the coals shift, sending yellow flames up the chimney, the fire crackling. She had the chair on one side of the hearth, Dad sat opposite in his work clothes of grey trousers and shirt, long legs stretched out in front of the fire. Tartan slippers. I liked to climb on his knee. My dad was dark, like my mum, but while she was small he was over six feet tall, with brown eyes. He had his hair cut regularly but in between going to the barber it grew just enough to curl up at the back over his collar. I loved his curls and kept asking him not to have them cut.

He'd look at me, eyes twinkling. 'You'd have me looking like a tramp, would you?'

I'd see him look across at my mother, his eyes bright, and I picked up on the warmth that passed between them. He never went out, my dad, not without Mum. There was no drinking, no coming in late from the pub. I'd heard my mum talk about her father coming home drunk, beating her mother, but I couldn't imagine what that was like. When Dad wasn't working, on the lookout with my brother for scrap metal, he was at home, legs at full stretch, in front of the fire. I knew they were happy, my parents. Every afternoon when it was getting close to the time for Dad coming in from work, Mum shooed us out of his armchair and put his slippers in the hearth to warm. A fresh pot of tea was made, as if by magic, the second he came through the door. On the table was crusty bread, fresh from the oven. The odd time he was late home, she was out in the street waiting for him. Worried. I saw all this. The way they were with each other when he came in, it was as if those few hours they were apart each day while he was at work were as much as either of them could bear. My parents loved each other. There was no shouting.

That came later.

As well as the scrap metal business, my dad had a stall down Walthamstow market selling flowers and fruit and vegetables. I used to go with him. I was only little, probably about eight, and to me it was a really exciting place, full of bustle. The coloured bulbs strung between the stalls made it look festive all year round. Opposite where my dad's stall was at the top of the high street was a couple who sold sarsaparilla by the glass. They wore white coats and their stall was spotless clean. I didn't really like the taste of sarsaparilla but I'd have a glass anyway, just because it seemed like something special, medicinal almost. Spending so much time in hospital had definitely had an effect. Thinking about it, maybe that was why I was so taken by the dolls' hospital on the high street. I used to stand for ages at the window staring at all the sad broken dolls waiting to be patched up. I still wasn't completely better and suffered with the rheumatism in my legs. When they got bad Mum would wrap them up and light a fire in my bedroom, pull the bed in front of it to keep me cosy. It was heaven lying there watching the logs burn down and shift in the grate.

If there was money about, we'd go to Manze's, the pie and mash shop, for dinner. Inside, it had tiled walls and booths with wooden tables and bench seats. I don't think it's changed that much since the nineteen-fifties when I first went there. Everything about the place seemed larger than life to me, even the knives and forks with heavy wooden handles. It was popular, especially on market day, and there'd be a queue to get in. The staff wore starched white coats and there was one woman – she might have been in charge – who always looked immaculate. She kept a lace trimmed hanky in the breast pocket of her coat, and had pretty makeup and short grey hair. She always looked as if she had just come from the hairdresser. The only thing I didn't like about Manze's was you'd see old people having jellied eels and spitting out the bones. The sight used to turn my stomach.

Eels were popular then and Mum sometimes sent me down the market to get them fresh from the stall. I dreaded it, seeing the eels in tanks, writhing and slithering about. The man on the stall was ruddy-faced and wore an apron that was covered in blood. For some reason I never worked out he had a rubber thimble on his thumb. He'd grab a wriggling eel from one of the tanks, slap it on the chopping board and hack its head off with a cleaver. Chop, chop. The poor thing's mouth would be opening and closing as he slit open the body and pulled out the guts. It made me feel sick. I'd run home holding the bag with the freshly-killed eel by my fingertips, keeping it as far away from me as I could. At home, my brother never seemed to tire of chasing me round the house with the head. I'm not a fussy eater but there are certain things I won't eat. Like eels. Or winkles. My dad would buy a pint of them from the market, bring them home in a brown paper bag and sit, scooping bits of slime from the shell with a pin, dipping them in vinegar. They never looked all that good to eat to me.

I liked rabbit. We had that a lot. More than anything I loved sweets. I still have a sweet tooth. The best market stall was Strutt's where they sold long candy twists and would cut a length for you with silver clippers. Mum would send me off for a pound and a half of Strutt's. Just the smell of the sweet stall was heaven to me.

My dad was easy-going most of the time. Once or twice he banged Lizzie's and Christine's heads together when their squabbling got too much, but that was about it. At the market, he'd send me down what he called the 'culfi' shop to get him a coffee. One particular day, I was coming through the busy market with his 'culfi' in an enamel mug, trying not to spill it, getting knocked and jostled all the way. By the time I made it back to the stall, most of the coffee had been spilled. He wasn't pleased and sent me home with a crate of oranges for my mother. I don't think my dad, a big bloke, realised how heavy the crate was for a skinny little thing like me. I struggled back through the market with it and got on a bus that took me as far as the bottom of St Andrew's Road. From there, I had to walk to Higham Hill and cross over to get to Hamilton Road. It was a long way for a child lugging a crate of oranges. It just so happened to be a baking hot summer day and I was in a little white sun dress embroidered in red. By the time I got off the bus I was drenched in sweat and the dress was like a rag, sticking to me, my long hair plastered to my head. I stood at the side of the road feeling terrible, taking big heaving breaths, thinking I was going to die. I got as far as the middle of Higham Hill before I had to put the crate down and sit on it while I got my breath back. How I found the strength to get home I really couldn't say. I was in a state, though, practically on my knees, by then. That night, Mum gave Dad a telling-off. It was the only time I heard her sounding cross with him.

5.

I was about nine when we moved to a council house in Forest Road, not all that far from Hamilton Road. There was a lot of talk about the new house, Mum saying things like, 'Can you imagine a kitchen where I don't have to keep going up and down stairs the whole time?' Dad took me to see the new place, a Victorian terraced property, and even from the outside it did look smart; no unused shop front for a start. Unlike my mum, I wasn't all that excited about moving. Kids take things in their stride, I suppose.

We had a dog at the time, a big scruffy thing. I don't remember much about him, just that my mum didn't want him coming to the new house with us.

'Take that dog down the police station and tell them it's been following you,' she said.

I did as I was told.

'This dog's following me,' I said. 'And we don't want it no more.'

The policeman looked at me. 'So it's not yours, then?'

I shook my head.

'It seems awful fond of you for a stranger.'

I ended up taking it back home.

The day we got the keys to the new house, Dad sent me and Gillian on ahead to open up. We took the dog with us. The house was like a palace. Downstairs, it had a living room with a fireplace – no central heating, not that we cared – and a kitchen, a proper one, nothing like our old scullery with its bare concrete floor and single tap. There was a bathroom off the kitchen and a separate toilet. No more tin bath. Everything felt bright and modern. At the back, we had a brick shed and a nice little garden. The dog went mental, barking, trying to get at it. Dad hadn't given us the key for the back door so we ended up opening a window and lifting the dog out. It made straight for a raised flower bed in the middle of the grass and ran round and round in circles like a mad thing, churning up the soil. Seeing the dog so happy, I was glad we'd kept him.

Upstairs, the first bedroom you came to had double doors. Up another two stairs were two more bedrooms. There were fewer of us at home by then and things were a bit easier, money-wise, for my parents. Mum was always baking. Not just a cake or a few scones but whole batches of things ... coconut cakes, currant buns, you name it. I'd be running down the road tossing a hot cake from one hand to the other waiting for it to cool down. I was still little enough to enjoy sitting on my dad's lap but all that stopped when Jean called round one day and had a go at him.

'She'll still be sitting on your knee when she's thirty,' she said, sneering.

I didn't know what she meant by that but Dad looked embarrassed and made me get down. From then on I was never allowed on his lap.

I loved the new house but I wasn't so keen on walking to school from there. Chatham Road was opposite and I had to go a little way down there and into Bunyan Road, then along Elizabeth Avenue to Higham Hill as far as the fish and chip shop on the corner. There were always big boys outside who'd shout 'gypsy' at me when I went past. It wasn't as if they even knew me but I had very long curly hair and gold earrings, so that must have been what set them off. Once past the chip shop a few side roads eventually took me to St Andrew's Road. It probably wasn't that far but it was definitely a longer walk than from the old house. In any case, it felt like a long way to me and I found it a bit scary.

I was nine and in Mr Oliver's class when I got ill again. I wasn't keen on Mr Oliver. He had bushy black eyebrows and big hairy hands that gave me the creeps. For PE we had to wear little white tops and navy knickers and he would put his hands inside the elastic at the tops of the legs of my knickers and give me this weird look. I couldn't stand it.

The day I got ill, I woke up feeling poorly. It was winter, cold outside. Mum told me to put my coat on but I was burning up and went out without it. When I got to school I felt awful. At break it was raining and Mr Oliver said we all had to run across the playground to the toilets and come back in again. My throat was sore and I was aching and I remember putting my head down on the desk, just wanting to feel the coolness of the wood against my cheek. In the end, Mr Oliver sent me home. I walked back on my own, dragging myself for what felt like miles. By the time I got to Forest Road I could hardly breathe. Dr Frederick came, checked me over, and called an ambulance. I was off again, bells ringing, all the way to Whipps Cross Hospital. They took me to Byron Ward and put me in a glass cubicle again. All of it – Dr Frederick, the ambulance, the cubicle – was exactly like it had been the last time.

There was some kind of Royal visit that day and nobody was interested in me. It felt like we were kept waiting for hours. Eventually my dad – one of the most placid men you could ever hope to meet – got hold of a doctor by the throat and demanded he take a look at me. Next thing, everybody was rushing about, frantic. My temperature was 106 and I was gasping for air, at death's door. I had double pneumonia. I'm not sure how long I was in hospital. Weeks, I think. I was so poorly my parents thought I wouldn't pull through and had a request played for me on the radio. I even got a get well card from the actor Charlie Drake. As I started to feel better and was allowed out of bed, Mum and Dad got me a little blue dressing gown with a white lamb embroidered on the breast pocket.

In hospital, one thing I used to dread were the regular visits from a man in a white coat to take blood. He carried a wooden case full of syringes and wore the kind of glasses that made his eyes look enormous. Soon as I caught sight of him I was off, scooting down to the doll's house at the end of the ward and hiding inside. He always knew where to find me.

On the same ward as me was another girl from my class,

Josephine Easton, who had kidney problems. Another classmate, Lorraine Vernon, ended up in the bed next to mine with appendicitis. A teacher used to come round and we'd all do sums together, keep up with our schoolwork a bit. I liked it on the ward. Some of the nurses were nuns and they were lovely. I was coming back from the bathroom one day and one of the nuns was with Lorraine when I came flying past and took a running jump onto my bed. The poor nun almost jumped out of her skin but all she did was laugh. She didn't tell me off, just gave me a tickling. The only person I didn't get on with was a crotchety cleaner who used to grumble and bash your bed with her broom. I never understood why she scattered damp tea leaves on the floor before sweeping up, and I never dared ask, but now I think they were a way of gathering up dust. Anyway, she was only ever nice to Josephine, whose parents seemed to be there all the time. I didn't know that Josephine was dangerously ill, although she had been off school a lot over the years. Once I saw her in hospital all those absences made sense. Poor girl, her kidney problems weren't going away. One morning I woke up and her bed was empty. Josephine had died during the night.

6.

I moved to Willowfield School when I was eleven. The
uniform was a pale blue blouse, royal blue cardigan, grey skirt,
grey blazer, black shoes. My poor mum didn't have the money
to get me a pair of proper school shoes but there was a boot
mender a couple of doors up from us so Mum took a pair of
my old white shoes and got him to do a repair job. I hated Mr
Russell's shop. It was smelly and filthy. I wasn't keen on Mr
Russell either. He was a horrible old man who sat at a bench in
the window watching all the children play out. I don't know
what had happened to him but he had no legs. It didn't matter
what kind of shoes you took in for repair by the time he'd
finished with them they looked like ugly, clumpy, orthopaedic
ones. He was known for it. If you'd had your shoes mended by
old Mr Russell you were in for a lot of name-calling. Words we
don't say any more. 'Cripple shoes.' That kind of thing. So,
when my old white shoes came back from the mender, they
had thick built-up soles. My mum decided to make them black
by giving them a coat of gloss paint. I had no choice but to

wear these awful monstrosities for school. Straight away, the leather started cracking and the white showed through. They weren't black for long.

All my sisters had been to Willowfield. When I started I made my mind up I was going to do well. My first day there, in the hall with all the other first years, waiting to be told which class I was in, I couldn't hear the teacher for this other new girl in front of me talking non-stop. I gave her a nudge.

'Will you shut up?'

She looked at me. Hard little face, dark curly hair.

'I'm going to get you outside,' she said.

'Good, but shut up now, will you? I can't hear what class I'm in.'

As we streamed out of the hall, she collared me.

'I'm going to be your best mate,' she said.

Her name was Mandy and we were in the same class. She was trouble. For all my good intentions, I'd got in with a bad girl straight away. I wasn't even out of the hall when the headmistress pulled me to one side.

'I've had to deal with all the Jones girls,' she said, frosty. 'I've got my eye on you.'

I had no idea what that she meant by that but before long before I found out. Having put up with all sorts from my sisters, she had it in for me.

I was doing well, in the top five of my class, managing to keep out of trouble, until one day I was coming through the hall as the Head was on her way down the spiral staircase that led from her office. She tripped, fell down the last few stairs, and landed with her legs in the air, big pink bloomers on show. I wasn't the only one laughing but I got singled out for the ruler. Everything I did seemed to land me in trouble. Even in pottery, when I tried to make a vase for my mum, it went wrong and wet clay went flying off the wheel, bits going everywhere, landing in the teacher's hair, splattering her face.

It was an accident but I got sent out.

I seemed to get sent out a lot.

When I was growing up I always wanted to be like my big sisters. They seemed very glamorous to me. Gillian would pin her hair up and leave it overnight so the next morning she had all these lovely curls. Lizzie kept her hair short and wavy at the back and was at the hairdresser every week getting it set. A dress she had, cream and very fitted, with a black bow at the front, sticks in my mind. I liked it so much I had one almost identical made a few years ago. Christine and Lizzie were slim with good figures, Lizzie proud of a stomach that was flat as an ironing board. She was always immaculate, hair and face done, dabbing musky scent behind her ears. I'd watch her do her makeup and go outside with a small compact mirror to check it in natural light, turning the mirror this way and that.

The smell that hung around the house – scent and smoke and alcohol – after a night out conjured up images for me of clubs packed with sophisticated people drinking and dancing and having a good time. I don't know where my sisters went on a night out but seeing them get ready was exciting to me. Years later, to my amazement, I found out that Lizzie was mixing with the gangsters, Reggie and Ronnie Kray, and that Reg was a good friend.

By the time I was twelve I was going out of my way to look grown-up, like my sisters. I had long hair, wore make up, had boobs, and a cigarette in one hand. I didn't really like smoking but everyone was doing it and cigarettes were easy to get hold of. A woman up the road from my friend, Hazel, sold us Player's Weights. No one ever told me that twelve was too young to be puffing away. Thinking about it, I probably was on the wild side but not in a thieving/swearing/causing trouble kind of way. Mostly, when I was out with my mates I was hanging about in the street, nothing bad. I'd get a telling-off for coming in late but more because Mum was waiting to lock up than anyone was worried something might have happened to me. I was allowed to do what I wanted, dress like my big sisters, so that's what I did. There's a photo of me when I was twelve in a green velvet dress, cigarette in hand, with one of my cousins, who was eighteen. You'd think it was me that was the adult, not the other way round. No one ever tried to make me look like the little girl I was. One day I was mistaken for my sister, Gillian, who was eighteen at the time. I might have looked the part but I was innocent as anything, green as grass.

I was out with my friend Maureen one night and we went off with some lads in a car. It wasn't as if they were strangers; I knew who they were. The lad whose car it was, Johnny Someone, was something to do with my friend Mandy's dad, which was good enough for me. He was very good-looking, Johnny, and funny. A nice bloke, I thought, doing alright for himself in his smart red car with cream leather seats. I was done up in one of my tight little dresses, stockings and high heels, and ended up in the car with him while Maureen went with his friend. Johnny lived in Tottenham and that's where he took me, back to his house. His grandparents lived there and his Mum had the upstairs done out as a kind of sitting room and bedroom all in one. I thought it was all right to go up with him even though there was no one in. I was being so grown-up. He was giving me drinks, something alcoholic I didn't like the taste of, and the next thing he was all over me pulling at my dress and I was shouting at him to stop.

He raped me.

I was crying, yelling, saying I was only twelve, and that freaked him out. He beat me up, slapped me round the face and told me I was a bloody little cow. I was still crying when he threw me out. I walked to the bottom of the road and got a bus that went round Tottenham Hale. The conductor gave me a look when he took my fare but didn't say anything. The bus took me so far and I walked the rest of the way home, catching sight of my reflection in a shop window. My face was battered-looking: black eye coming up, split ear, bloody mouth.

Mum and Dad and Patricia were watching telly when I got in. For once, I wasn't late. I went in the living room.

Mum looked up. 'Look at the state of you.'

Patricia gave me a look of disgust. 'Little cow, who's she been upsetting now?'

No one asked what had happened and I didn't say. I went upstairs and got into bed with my clothes on and lay in the dark wishing I could die, thinking what had happened was my fault. Tears ran down my face. My body shook. Every bit of me was hurting. I hated myself. I didn't blame Johnny. It was *me*. I'd done this. Round and round my head went the same thought: 'Serves you right.'

I was thinking if everyone kept telling me what a little cow I was, it had to be true. I was bad, disgusting. I really believed it. It's only now, years later, I've worked out that what that boy did to me that night wasn't my fault. I wasn't a little cow. I was an innocent mixed-up child who couldn't work out who she was or how she was meant to behave. At home, half the time I was the baby and the other half a selfish little cow. I didn't appreciate how grown-up I looked or the kind of trouble it could land me in and no one ever told me how to take care of myself. There was no discipline. If I wanted to go out dressed to kill, smoke, have the odd drink, it was up to me. My sisters thought it was funny, me looking older than my years. I remember Christine staying over and making some remark about not trusting me with Bob, her husband. I was a kid, twelve years old. I didn't know what she was getting at.

Despite what everyone thought, I wasn't half as grown-up as I looked.

When I think about it, my parents must have been exhausted by the time they had me. I was their sixth daughter, after all. They were probably a lot stricter with the others but when it came to me I don't think they had it in them any more to lay down the law. Instead, they turned a blind eye and hoped for the best, and most of the time it was OK, them not asking, me not telling.

I never told a soul about being raped.

It was a secret I kept for fifty years.

7.

I ran all the way home. Late. Again. As I tore along Forest Road I tripped on a bit of uneven pavement and almost went flying in my heels. Not the best shoes for running. I took them off and kept going in my stocking feet, picturing Mum in her dressing gown, waiting up, livid. The night before she'd given me what she called a final warning. I had to be in by ten o'clock. Or else. She'd had enough of me keeping her up night after night when she was ready for bed, she said. It was driving her round the bend.

It wasn't as if I was doing it on purpose or that I was even all that late. Ten minutes. Fifteen, maybe. It wouldn't have taken much to do as I was told and get home on time, keep on her good side. Why I couldn't, I have no idea. Whenever she put me on the spot and wanted to know what was so important I had to be out late night after night I couldn't think what to say, so I kept quiet. It was no good trying to explain that once I was with my mates, chatting, having a smoke, I lost all sense of time. It was like I was in another world. Mum would have gone, 'I'll give you another world,' and landed me one. At thirteen, I still felt the weight of her hand when I got on the wrong side of her.

When I got to the front door my heart was thudding so hard I thought it would burst. I hung back on the doorstep, doubled up with a stitch in my side, getting my breath back. Then I knocked. The look on Mum's face when she opened up told me I was for it.

'What time do you call this? Get in the house!' she said.

I was about to go straight up to bed but she wasn't having it. 'Get in that living room, Jenny.'

The fire was out and the room was chilly. On the table next to Mum's chair was a cup and saucer. She stood with her arms crossed, looking me up and down.

I was holding my shoes. There was a big ladder up the front of my stockings. I must have ripped them when I was running.

'What the bloody hell have you been doing?'

I hadn't been doing anything. Hanging round with me mates, sitting on a wall round the corner from Fat June's house, Fat June going on like she always did about how she couldn't work out why she was so big. Mandy saying it might have something to do with stuffing her face with Kit Kats. Fat June looking put out, saying that wasn't it, she hardly ate a thing, and Mandy rolling her eyes – her way of saying pull the other one. Me keeping out of it. That was all we'd been doing. Talking. Smoking a couple of cigarettes. I shrugged.

Mum wasn't in the mood. 'Little cow. Don't think you're too big for a slap.'

I kept my eyes down. My stockings were ruined.

'If I have to ask you one more time what you're doing stopping out night after night …'

I looked up. Her face was drawn. My mum, always so smart and glamorous-looking with her little suits and heels and lovely black hair, seemed to have shrunk all of a sudden. In her night things she looked done in, and it went through my head that it was down to me. I was putting years on her.

'Who've you been with? What you getting up to?' She gave me a long look. 'Are you pregnant?'

Pregnant. She might as well have slapped me across the face. 'No! I'm not pregnant!'

She kept her eyes on me. 'You'd better not be.'

I felt tears well up. Was that what she thought of me? She couldn't have been more wrong. After what that older lad had done, raped and beaten me, no way would I let boys anywhere near. Just because I wore make-up and short skirts and had plenty of mates didn't mean I was cheap. I knew where she'd got the idea – Patricia. Slouched on the sofa in her tatty old dressing gown with a rip under the arm, spitting poison the whole time. In her twisted mind there could only be one reason for my being popular; I had to be sleeping around.

'You don't want to believe everything Fatty Arbuckle tells you,' I said, getting upset. 'That jealous cow.'

I wished I could tell Mum about the lad who'd attacked me. I couldn't, though. Couldn't say a thing about it. Not when deep down I blamed myself for what had happened.

'At least I know what your sister's doing,' Mum was saying.

'At least I've got mates! No one wants to hang round with her!' I was shouting now.

Mum bent down, picked up the tea cup from the table and chucked it at me. It went flying past my head and smashed against the wall. Cold tea ran down the paintwork. I was so shocked I couldn't move. Before I knew it she had the saucer in her hand. Just in time, I ducked out of the way. It went the same way as the cup and shattered. All along the mantelpiece were brass ornaments. Before she could get hold of one I turned and fled up the stairs to bed. My heart was thumping again. When I put my hand on my chest I felt it racing. I'd had a few run-ins with Mum but never seen her so cross. I got into bed thinking about the cup and saucer flying across the room. She would feel bad about that in the morning.

It was her best china.

I called for Mandy on the way to school. Her house backed onto the playground so what we did was wait until the last minute then ran across when the bell went. Mandy lived with her dad, who let her run wild. He couldn't care less what time she came in. As long as she was home before he got back from the pub with whoever his latest girlfriend was he was none the wiser.

'What happened to you?' she said.

I had scratches all down one side of my face.

'I had a fight with Patricia.'

That morning she was at the table slurping down her cereal when I told her I was sick of her dropping me in it with Mum. Called her a fat slob. Said she was jealous and no lad would want to touch her with a barge pole. That was when she came flying out of her seat, almost knocking me over, and raked her nails down my face. I hit her back, right in the gut. She didn't seem to notice. I swung another punch, harder. It didn't do a thing. Mum heard the commotion and ran in to split us up. It was always me, the little one, Mum got hold of. Once she'd got me in a headlock I couldn't move, couldn't even defend myself, while Patricia kept on whacking me in the face.

'Leave off, will you?' Mum kept saying, tightening her grip. 'Leave *off*, you little cow.'

I wouldn't care, it was me she was talking to.

I told Mandy about the row the night before, the best china getting smashed. Mum must have cleaned it up before going to bed because there was no sign of it when I got up. Mandy rolled her eyes in that way of hers.

'I wouldn't put up with any of that,' she said.

It was easy for her to say. Her mum had walked out years before, and with her dad at work or in the pub and hardly ever in, it wasn't like anyone was keeping tabs on her. She gave me a cigarette from a pack her dad had bought in the pub the night before and forgotten about. He liked a drink, her dad. Most of the time he was so far gone he never noticed when his fags went missing, which was handy for us. I looked at Mandy. Thirteen, going on thirty. She got away with murder.

The living room reeked of booze and stale smoke. The curtains were still shut from the night before. Mandy didn't bother opening them.

'There's a film on this afternoon,' she was saying, blowing smoke up at the discoloured ceiling. 'Shall we stay in and watch it?'

I didn't much feel like going to school. I had geography

first thing, a subject I hated. It wasn't so much the geography, more the teacher I couldn't stand. Miss Reynolds wasn't keen on me either. The week before she'd been talking about a country I'd never heard of, spinning the globe at the front of the classroom to show us where it was. For some reason she hoisted the thing off its stand and held it up. One of the other girls was talking at the back but it was me Miss Reynolds told off. If she caught me again, she said, she would chuck the globe at me. It looked heavy, like it would flatten you, so I didn't answer back. In any case, I wanted to know where Suriname, the country she was talking about, was. South America, it turned out, on the north east coast, just down from Venezuela. As she was putting the globe back on its stand it slipped out of her hand and fell on her foot. The sound it made, it had to have hurt. Everyone gasped. Miss Reynolds went a funny colour. She spun round and glared at me – as if it was my fault. I couldn't help it, I started laughing. Next thing, she was hobbling towards me looking ready to commit murder. For someone with a crushed foot she didn't half move fast. She was almost on top of me when I made a run for it, dodging round the desks and out the door. I was sprinting off down the corridor when I heard her bellowing, 'Come back here, Jennifer Jones!'

I didn't stop until I got home.

Next day, I got thrashed with the ruler for that.

Mandy and me settled down on the sofa and smoked our way through half her dad's cigarettes. In no time, the air in the living room was thick with smoke. I wondered if we should open a window, clear the air a bit.

'Doesn't he ever notice his cigarettes keep disappearing?' I said.

Mandy gave a toss of her head. 'He brought some woman back last night. Sitting having a cup of tea like she owned the place this morning.'

One night I'd stayed over at Mandy's and the pair of us were asleep when the light went on and there was her dad, smelling like a brewery, some blonde woman in a tatty car coat beside him. 'This is so-and-so,' he was saying, as the woman, bleary-eyed, every bit as drunk as he was, hung on his arm.

Mandy had sat up in bed, squinting into the light. 'Put that off, will you? I've got my friend Jenny staying,' she said, frosty enough to send the pair of them packing, full of apologies.

It was about four o'clock when I set off for home. I wanted to get back in my mum's good books and the best way to do that was to keep my head down. I wouldn't go out for a bit, I decided. Make more of an effort to do as I was told. And, as much as I could, I'd keep out of Patricia's way.

When I got home there were a couple of bin liners full of stuff on the step. I knocked at the door. I wished Mum would just let me have my own key. I had to knock again before Patricia opened up. She blocked my way.

'There's your stuff,' she said, nodding at the bags. 'Now you can eff off.'

I tried to push past. She shoved me back. 'Don't think you're getting in, you little trollop.'

I shouted for Mum. I knew she was inside. She always had the kettle on, fresh pot of tea on the go, when I got home from school.

'She's had it up to here with you,' Patricia said. 'We all have. So clear off, and take your stuff with you.' She aimed a kick at one of the bags and it tipped up. My good top, white with a scoop neck and little puff sleeves, fell out.

I snatched it up and tried to barge my way in. Patricia, twice my size, filled the doorframe, stopping me.

'Mum! Mum!'

'Shout all you want, you little cow. She's not coming.'

'MUM!'

Patricia took a step forward. 'If I have to tell you one more time you won't know what's hit you.'

I stood holding my top, no idea what to do, and it went through my head that Mum must have packed my stuff. She had to be inside now, hearing all the shouting, waiting for me to go. I knew things were bad the night before, but this … I picked up the bin bags and turned away. The door slammed shut behind me.

I headed back along the road, not knowing where I was going, feeling like I'd swallowed a brick. The bags were heavy. The heel of a shoe poked through one of them. At the end of the street I stopped, pushed it back inside, and thought for a minute about what to do. I wondered about going back. Maybe Mum would let me in this time. No, not if Patricia had anything to do with it. I kept going and got a bus to Tottenham where my friend Barbara lived.

'Blimey, Jenny, what you got there?' Barbara said, when she opened the door and saw the bin bags.

'I've been chucked out.'

She pulled the door shut behind her. 'What you going to do?'

'Don't suppose I could stop here for a bit?'

She made a face. 'We've got no room.'

Her house was full of kids, the way ours used to be. We sat on the doorstep for a bit, not saying anything.

'I've thought of something,' Barbara said, eventually.

Her brother had a car, a blue and white Triumph Herald. Barbara pleaded with him to let me sleep in it. 'She's got nowhere else to go,' she said.

It was obvious he wasn't keen. Neither was I but I didn't have much choice. Barbara sneaked me a pillow and a spare blanket and we put my belongings in the boot. I don't think I slept at all the first night, hunched up on the back seat. I couldn't get warm and when the heavens opened in the early hours the sound of rain on the roof was deafening. In the morning, I was full of aches and pains and felt grubby. I had to make do with a quick wash at school. That night, I was back in the Herald, tossing and turning. A group of lads coming down the road after closing time banged on the back window and frightened the life out of me. For the rest of the night I sat bolt upright, wide awake. I couldn't face a third night.

My friend, Maureen, came to the rescue.

'You can't sleep in a car!' she said, when I told her what was going on. 'Come home with me and I'll ask Mum if you can stay with us.'

Maureen had a lovely bedroom, all to herself. It was done out in pink and white with twin beds next to each other, a little table and a lamp in between. Each bed had a padded velvet headboard and matching covers with frilly edging. It seemed to me the height of luxury and a world away from home, where some nights I'd drag my mattress along the landing and sleep outside my parents' room, just to get away from Patricia. I stretched out on Maureen's bed for a minute and shut my eyes. I was thirteen and homeless. Was I really so bad my mother had to throw me out? Patricia had called me a trollop. I didn't even know what it meant but it had to be something bad. Maureen had a bookcase in the corner of the room. On the bottom shelf next to a dozen *Famous Five* books was a dictionary. I sat on the floor and looked up trollop. *Disreputable girl or woman.* I looked up disreputable. *Having a bad reputation; not respectable.* I put the dictionary back on the shelf. I took *trollop* to mean that Patricia thought I was sleeping around and my mum did too. I felt like crying, thinking about that older lad forcing himself on me. It was Maureen I'd been out with that night and I still hadn't said a word about what had happened. I wasn't going to either. The bedroom door opened.

'Mum says you can stay here tonight, see what happens tomorrow,' Maureen said.

One night became two, then a week. I didn't hear a word from my mum. I was really missing her. One day I came home from school and there was a letter waiting for me in an official-looking brown envelope. It was from Social Services, saying I was too young to have left home and had to attend a meeting with a social worker on such and such a date. Mum must have been in touch with them. And Maureen's mum must have been in touch with her, otherwise how did the Social know where I was? I didn't know what to make of the letter. The way it was worded you'd have thought I'd upped and left of my own accord when the truth was I'd been booted out. For the next couple of days I carried the letter round with me, wondering what would happen next. A few days before the meeting was due Mum got in touch and asked me to go round and have dinner with her and Dad. I'd been gone a couple of weeks by then. When I knocked at the door it was Mum who came to let me in. No sign of Patricia. The smell coming from the kitchen was lovely. Chicken in gravy, mashed potatoes, some of that crusty bread Mum made, straight out of the oven. We sat down, the three of us, and had our dinner. I'd always loved Mum's cooking and ate every mouthful, mopping up the gravy with a piece of warm bread. Mum asked about school. Dad kept quiet. I don't think he said a single word. There was no mention of what had happened, or Social Services, or what I was doing living with one of my friends.

'We want you to come home, Jenny,' Mum said, as she cleared the plates away.

I didn't need asking twice. I went back to Maureen's, packed my stuff into the bin bags, and got the bus home.

8.

Every night Patricia waited until I'd been in bed a few minutes and was almost asleep before starting on me.

'Shut up, Jenny, shut UP!'

I would practically jump out of my skin.

'You're shouting out, you little cow. How am I supposed to get any sleep with all that going on?'

Was I? I'd settle down and lie there, wide awake, not making a sound. A few minutes later, Patricia was off again.

'Will you SHUT UP!'

I started to think I must be going mad if I was making a racket without even knowing I was doing it. It got so I couldn't stand being yelled at and would haul my mattress onto the landing to get some peace. One night Christine was visiting and the fog was bad so she couldn't get home and had to share my bed. Patricia had already turned in and didn't know about Christine staying over. Soon as we got into bed Patricia was off, yelling at me to shut up. She must have got the shock of her life when Christine told her to cut it out.

'Jenny wasn't doing nothing,' Christine said the next morning when she told Mum what had been going on.

I thought that would be the end of it but it made no difference. A few nights later, Patricia was up to her old tricks again and I was back on the landing. At least now I knew I wasn't going mad.

In the morning, Patricia would complain to Mum that I'd kept her awake. When I said it was Fatty Arbuckle stirring things, there'd be another fight. Every day I went out with bruises, scratches on my face. Plenty of times I bunked off school and hung about with Mandy, smoking and watching telly.

Even though I was skipping lessons I was keeping up and was in the top set for everything. When we had tests I did all right, usually coming in the top five. The headmistress still had me in her sights, though. Every time she saw me she'd pull me up, often because I was wearing make-up.

'Go and wash that stuff off your face,' she'd say.

One day I had no make-up on and she still collared me. 'I'm not having you coming to school looking like you're going to a nightclub,' the headmistress said. 'Go and wash your face and then report back to me.'

I went to the toilets where some of the other girls were washing their makeup off, and hung around for a bit, had a cigarette. Then I went back to see the Head.

'That's more like it. You must feel better now,' she said.

'Yes, Miss.'

After break one morning, Mandy said she'd race me back to class. When the bell went I took off across the playground, through the swing doors and along the corridor. I was miles in front when I slipped and skidded headfirst on my belly. I came to a halt inches from a pair of sensible brown lace-ups. The headmistress. I got to my feet.

'In my office, now,' she said.

She gave me the ruler and a long speech I'd heard before about the trouble she'd had from the Jones girls over the years and how she wasn't having it with me. All the time she was telling me off I was thinking about Mandy, wondering how come she hadn't got caught.

'Since you can't behave I'm putting you in the bottom set,' the Head was saying.

I stared at her. No one called it the bottom set. 'What, with the *dunces*?'

She gave me a stern look. 'Perhaps you'll learn to think more carefully about the consequences of your actions,' she said. 'Go on, back to your class for now.'

I left her office in a daze. The dunces. The dregs of the school. The ones who would never make anything of themselves. Even Mandy, who was a real bad girl, wasn't in the bottom set. I couldn't be lumped in with that lot.

At lunchtime I went with Mandy back to her place.

'You should have climbed in the window, like I did,' she said, lighting up. 'Old droopy drawers wouldn't have caught you then.'

We didn't bother going back in the afternoon.

I was in the bottom set for two weeks. I hated it. The teachers were up in arms about my being there. One or two took me to one side – even Miss Reynolds, who couldn't stand me – and said they'd do what they could to sort things out. I might not have been a model pupil but I was bright and it grated on the teachers seeing me in a class where no one had the slightest intention of learning anything. Whatever went on behind the scenes, the Head changed her mind, and I went back into the top set. By then, I'd decided I wasn't staying on at school a minute longer than I had to – and I certainly wasn't going to stick around to take my exams. For the next year or so I played up and bunked off and did what I liked. I was hardly ever there. One day I walked into a maths class for the first time in weeks and the teacher said, 'Oh, Jennifer Jones, we *are* honoured. What's been the problem – a pain in your little finger?'

'No,' I said, 'one in me big toe.'

'Out!'

I turned on my heel and left. I hadn't even got as far as my desk.

The earliest I could leave school was fifteen but a few months before my birthday Mum took pity on me and said I didn't have to go back. The school must have decided to turn a blind eye because nothing was ever said.

I left without a single qualification.

9.

My dad was always a gentle giant until he got ill. Mum was in the kitchen one day making tea, Dad in the living room, when there was an almighty crash. She went running and found him collapsed on the floor, one side of his face drooping. It looked like he'd had a stroke. Mum phoned for an ambulance, then knelt beside him, stroking his face, comforting him as best she could, until it got there. The whole time he didn't move, didn't say a thing. She told me later she thought he was a goner. It turned out he'd had a cerebral thrombosis – a clot on the brain. He was in Whipps Cross Hospital for weeks. I suppose that was when I first noticed a gruffness about him that hadn't been there before but put it down to him not liking being in hospital. He grumbled no end that the nurses who bathed him were far too young. 'Barely any older than you!' he'd say, mortified, when I went in to see him. Once he got home it was months before he was well enough to go back to work with my brother, doing the scrap metal. I don't think he was ever really right again. Just getting up out of the chair took it out of him. It was painful seeing him struggle to do the simplest thing. He was terrible on his legs and kept having falls. From being big and strong he became so unsteady he needed a stick to get about. He also seemed to be taking a lot of pills. The bathroom cabinet was full of them. All this happened around my fifteenth birthday when I was a typical selfish teenager, too wrapped up in my own life to worry about him. I thought he was invincible, that he would get better. He was my big strong dad, after all. It turned out I was wrong. From being mild, someone who never had much to say, all of a sudden he had a ferocious temper.

It didn't take much to set him off.

One night I was in front of the mirror in the living room getting ready to go out, checking my make-up and putting spray on my hair. In the chair behind me, Dad was reading the paper. I kept hearing him grunt and tut but took no notice until he was cursing.

'What the *effing hell?*'

I swung round to see him get to his feet, levering himself up with his stick. It seemed to take an age. When he finally turned to face me his glasses were all sticky and fogged up. He took them off, stared at them for a few seconds, baffled. Straight away I knew what had happened. His specs were covered in my hairspray. No wonder he was having a hard time reading the paper. I burst out laughing.

'Jesus! Fuck me! Hooray!' he sputtered, when the penny dropped.

For reasons none of us could fathom, ever since he got ill, the odd-sounding triple expletive was what he came out with whenever he lost his rag. It always cracked me up. I laughed even harder. I could see he was furious and that me doubled up wasn't helping matters. He took a few unsteady steps to the dining table, dropped his stick, picked up a chair and lifted it above his head to throw at me. For a second or two I couldn't move. From the thunderous look on his face I knew he was serious. Before he had a chance to lob the chair I made a run for it.

'And get that muck off your face!' he yelled, as I dodged past.

He'd never been shouty, my dad. Never raised a finger to me. Being ill was what made him like that. I hated it. My lovely, gentle dad, cursing and swearing.

It got so I didn't like being in the same room as him.

10.

'You need to get that Jenny working,' Mum told Patricia, once I'd turned fifteen.

Patricia had a job at a factory on Ferry Lane, a ten-minute walk from where we lived. My sister, Gillian, worked at the same place. I had no idea what the work involved but since I needed to start earning I was more than happy to be taken on, on the say-so of my sisters. I didn't even need an interview. At that time, with no experience or qualifications, jobs were still easy enough to come by.

On my first day I put on a little suit and did my hair and make-up. Patricia looked me up and down.

'Where do you think you're going, Miss High and Mighty?'

'A girl's got to make an effort,' I said, giving her a pointed look.

The factory was on a sprawling estate full of grey warehouses, not far from where we lived. All I knew about the job I'd be doing was that it was something to do with the jewellery trade. That didn't sound too bad. It turned out we were gluing pieces of velvet onto pads designed to display rings and necklaces and what not. The women worked at benches at one end of the factory, with a glue pot over a fire in front of them, while at the far end men operated heavy machinery. I never did find out what they were doing. The place was vast and all the machines going the whole time made an awful noise. What really hit me, though, was the overpowering stench of the glue. Sour and fishy, it was sickening. No one else seemed to mind. I suppose it was something you got used to.

The women wore overalls, shapeless housecoats. Mine just about tripped me up. Patricia was supposed to be training me but left me to my own devices. I hadn't a clue what I was doing so I watched the others and did my best to copy them. Opposite, was an older woman, Phyllis, with dark little eyes like raisins and a rigid shampoo-and-set. She made it look easy, dabbing the back of the velvet with just the right amount of glue, expertly attaching it to the backing plates. I dipped my brush in the glue pot. It was trickier to handle than it looked and I managed to get a few drops on the good side of the velvet, ruining it. Patricia made a tutting sound.

I started again, cutting another piece. Somehow I'd got glue on the bench and when I turned the velvet over it was all marked again. I gave it a rub. Now I had glue on my hands. I put the brush down next to my scissors. Next thing, they were covered as well.

'You want to give your scissors a clean,' Phyllis suggested, 'or they'll seize up.'

I watched her cutting and pasting and sticking and making it look effortless while I struggled on. I was so busy looking at her while I tried to get the glue off my scissors I managed to put the blade through my thumb. Blood ran onto the bench.

'Oh, for God's sake, watch what you're doing,' Patricia said, snatching up her work, afraid I might bleed on it.

'There's some plasters in the ladies,' Phyllis said, being helpful.

I hadn't made the best start.

At break time, we all trooped into the toilets. They reminded me of the changing rooms at school, with pegs along the walls to hang your coat, and rows of bench seats. Phyllis lit up. I noticed the index finger on her right hand stuck straight out. She caught me looking.

'Me stiff finger,' she said, holding it up. 'Occupational hazard. Comes from working with glue.'

I couldn't tell if she was having me on.

She was saying she'd been at the factory longer than she cared to remember and seen loads of young girls come and go, when I spotted something on the far side of the room. A rat was squeezing itself through the narrow gap at the bottom of the door. I gave Phyllis a dig and pointed, alarmed, as it scurried across the floor, inches from where we sat, before disappearing into one of the toilet cubicles. My stomach turned over.

'Oh, we get loads of them,' Phyllis said, dragging on her cigarette, not the least bit bothered.

That first week, my work kept coming back. I couldn't seem to get the hang of things. Patricia's idea of training involved nothing more than making sarcastic comments when I got things wrong. I sat at the bench, hating the sickly smell of the glue, fascinated by Phyllis and her stiff finger, keeping an eye out for rats, expecting to be fired any minute. How I wasn't, I'll never know, and when Friday came and I got my first wage packet it was all worthwhile. A little brown envelope with five crisp one pound notes inside. It was a lot of money to me. I went home and gave Mum two pounds for my keep. The other three were for me to spend on whatever I wanted. I felt so grown up, a world away from school.

I hadn't been at the factory long when we moved to new premises further away, on Farringdon Road. It meant getting the train from St James Street station, in Walthamstow. Every morning, I set off for work at the same time as Patricia, who hurried along leaving me trailing a few paces behind. At the station, she waited to see which carriage I got into and picked a different one. Sometimes, I'd get back out and get in hers, just to see the look on her face. Anyone watching would never have guessed we were sisters. I only lasted a few weeks at the new place before they sacked me after many more mishaps. It was obvious I was never going to get the hang of it.

The only thing I missed was Phyllis and her stiff finger.

11.

Opposite us on Forest Road was a tyre fitting place. One day, I was walking past with me mum when a few of the blokes that worked there were outside on a tea break. A voice said, 'Good morning, Jenny,' and I looked up to see the most handsome man I had ever set eyes on smiling at me. Tall, blond, blue-eyed. I was knocked sideways. It was more than just his good looks that got me. He had something else – charisma, I suppose I'd call it now. I couldn't believe someone like him would notice me, or know who I was.

I'd got a job on the petrol pumps at a garage on Markhouse Road, a few streets away, and I'd see him driving past. Just the sight of him was enough to turn me inside out. I asked around and found out he was called Nick Benson. When he came in for petrol it was always me that served him, even though being around him made me so dizzy I almost passed out. He was the loveliest thing and I was mad about him. Weeks went by and he still hadn't asked me out.

'Maybe he doesn't fancy me,' I said to Sue, who worked

with me.

'I bet he does,' she said.

'So why hasn't he said anything?'

She shrugged. 'Maybe he's waiting for the right moment.'

We came up with a plan so that the next time he came in Sue would ask if I was going up the road to get some milk from the machine, and I'd say I didn't fancy walking up there … in the hope Nick would offer me a lift.

Sure enough, a day or two later he came in, I served him, Sue said about the milk and I pulled a face. As luck would have it, it had just started raining.

'I'll take you,' he said, giving me a smile that made my insides flip over.

I got in his car, so shy I couldn't think of a thing to say. I hoped he'd think my silence was me being aloof rather than tongue-tied.

We drove up the road as far as the milk machine. On the way back, he said, 'What you doing on Saturday? Want to go for a drink?'

When he dropped me off, I went back into the kiosk and waited for him to drive away before collapsing against the wall. 'He only asked me out!'

I spent half the day getting ready for our date. I'd got a new little suit, a waistcoat and skirt in a lovely red crepe material. It was beautiful. I had a white blouse with a sweetheart neckline and laces up the front, and a pair of black patent chisel-toed boots. I thought I looked the business. When Nick came to pick me up Mum asked him in and showed him into the front room, which we only ever used for guests. He looked gorgeous, like a film star, in a light coloured suit and open-neck shirt. Suede boots. I still couldn't believe someone like him could be interested in little me. When we got in the car he asked where I fancied going; somewhere noisy or quiet. I didn't mind where we went. Being with him was enough for me.

He suggested driving out to a country pub at High Beach, in Epping.

'Don't worry, I won't stop the car in a quiet spot and misbehave or anything,' he said, giving me one of those smiles of his, as we set off.

I shot him a sideways look, thinking I wouldn't mind if he did.

On the way, I found out he was three years older than me, the only boy in a house full of girls, like my brother – and mad on cars. His two-tone Ford Consul, red and cream, roomy, with a leather interior and bench seat in the front, was his pride and joy.

'So, how old are you?' he said once we were settled at a table in a lovely old pub.

My sixteenth birthday was coming up in a few weeks.

'What date's your birthday?' he said.

When I told him June 14 he smiled. 'That's my birthday.' He would be nineteen.

I thought he was having me on. 'No!'

He nodded. 'What are the chances of that?' he said.

Silly as it may sound, it felt like a sign to me that we were meant for each other.

I reckon I was already a bit in love with him before we even had our first date. He was the first person I'd felt like that about. Until then, I'd kept boys at arms-length, going out with them but never letting anyone close. After what had happened to me when I was twelve I was so wary. I must have given the impression of being out of reach without even knowing it because the blokes that worked with Nick at the tyre fitting place reckoned he'd never get a date with me. With him, from the off, I felt different. I got butterflies just thinking about him. When we were together I was in heaven. Every waking moment, he was on my mind. I dreamed about him. Lived and breathed him. I knew he was the only one for me.

In the summer he went on holiday with a mate for a week in a caravan on the coast somewhere near Yarmouth. It had all been arranged before we started seeing each other. Every night he was gone he phoned and told me he loved me and missed me. I ached for him to come back. Not long after he did we were sitting in the pub one night and he started talking about us getting married.

'I missed you so much,' he said, giving my hand a squeeze. 'Let's save up, get married.'

I was the happiest I'd ever been. Nick made me feel safe. He was kind and gentle and treated me with respect. There was almost an innocence about him. The way he looked at me, those blue eyes going right through me, you'd have thought I was the only girl in the world. Yet I still had my moments when I struggled to get my head round what someone as extraordinary as him saw in me, a young girl barely out of school.

Mum seemed to have gone a bit cold on him and I couldn't work out why, not when she could see how happy I was. One night I brought him back for a coffee and we curled up on the sofa and fell asleep. That was all. Nothing went on. I suppose it must have got late and Mum came downstairs looking for me, saw the pair of us like that, and leapt to conclusions.

'What do you think you're doing?' she said, furious. We jumped up, bleary-eyed. 'It's not a doss house!'

She practically threw him out. I tried telling her we weren't up to anything but she wasn't interested. 'You need to watch your step with that one,' she said, stomping back upstairs to bed.

It was too late for that. I was already hooked.

Now and then, Nick would arrange to take me out and not turn up. The look on Mum's face let me know what she thought about him letting me down, although she never said much. It wasn't as if he stood me up without a word. If he couldn't make it he always phoned. Usually, it was car trouble. The Consul he was so fond of didn't half break down a lot. On New Year's Eve, 1968, we were going to a pub in Hackney to see a band and I was really looking forward to it. I'd got a new white dress with ostrich feathers, and a short red suede coat with a wide belt and big gold buckle. I pulled out all the stops getting ready. It was a big night and I wanted to look my best.

At eight o'clock the phone rang and Mum answered. Nick, saying he'd been held up but wouldn't be long. I stood at the front window in my new red coat looking out for him. An hour went by. Mum came in.

'Take your coat off, Jenny, and come and sit in the other room.'

I wouldn't. I knew he'd be there any minute.

It was midnight before I gave up. I sat on the sofa in my new coat crying while Mum did her best to console me.

'It's not the end of the world,' she said. 'You don't want to get yourself in a state over some boy.'

It wasn't some boy, though. I wanted to tell her it was serious with Nick, that I wanted to marry him. I kept quiet, though, since I had a good idea what she'd have to say about that.

The next day, he was round first thing, full of apologies. He'd done a mate a good turn, taken him out Epping way, and the car had packed up on the way back. The starter motor had gone. Or the fan belt. I wasn't sure. The way he told it, it got awful complicated. Anyway, it took him hours to get the car going again and by then it was gone midnight. He felt terrible, leaving me stranded on New Year's Eve.

'I'll make it up to you,' he said. 'We'll have our own celebration, something special, just the two of us.'

We did too. He took me to the pub we'd been to on our first date and I got to wear the dress with the ostrich feathers, and the red coat with the big gold buckle. It was a perfect night.

Even the Consul managed to behave.

12.

A couple of months later I was working at the garage one Saturday when I saw Nick drive past. He was in a cream suit and there were ribbons on his car. I looked at Sue.

'Did you see that? He never said he was going to a wedding,' I said.

I hadn't spoken to him for a couple of days. The night before when I was out with my mates he'd kept phoning, driving Mum mad, leaving messages. In the end he'd asked her to tell me he'd call in at the garage the following afternoon.

I was on the forecourt filling up a car when I saw him go past again, an hour or so later, this time in the opposite direction. Beside him, in the passenger seat, in a wedding dress and veil, was his ex-girlfriend, Lisa. I did a double take as the car cruised past, nice and slow, giving me time to get a good look at Lisa's happy face. Nick never so much as glanced in my direction. I felt sick as it dawned on me what I'd just seen. The ribbons on the car. Him in a suit. Lisa in a wedding dress. All that was missing was a 'just married' sign on the back of the car.

He'd been at a wedding, all right – his own!

Sue did what she could to calm me down. 'You don't know for definite, not until you ask him,' she said, putting an arm round me.

I was crying so much I could hardly speak. 'Ask him *what*? He just went past with the bride in the car,' I stuttered.

Sue tried again. 'What if he was just giving her a lift? He might have been.'

I stared at her. She went red and made a face. 'I mean … well, stranger things happen.'

If they did, I couldn't think of any. In the space of a few seconds, the bottom had gone crashing out of my world. I sat in the kiosk shaking, drinking the tea Sue made for me, my heart breaking.

I knew about Lisa. Nick had been going out with her before he started seeing me. It had been over between them for ages but she wouldn't leave him alone, he said. Some nights he'd get in from work and find her in the house drinking tea with his mum, crying. She took to hanging about at the bus stop over the road from where he lived. Once or twice, he spotted her in the local corner shop when he called in for cigarettes. A few times, he'd had to give her a lift home just to get rid of her. I'd seen her in the car with him before.

'She's doing my head in,' he used to say. 'I'm sick of telling her. She won't get the message.'

She sounded obsessed, crazy. I had some sympathy because I'd look at him and could see why she wouldn't want to let him go. I felt like the luckiest person alive to have him. Now, thinking about it, I wondered if everything he'd told me had been lies. If he'd been seeing her all along. The thought turned my stomach. I went to the toilet and threw up. In the mirror I looked awful. Pale, red-eyed, mascara smudged. I washed my face as best I could and tidied up my hair. I still had to finish my shift before I went home.

For the next few hours, all I could think about was Nick. And Lisa. The sight of them going past in their wedding gear was running on a loop inside my head. The more I thought about it the worse I felt. I had a pain in my chest, as if someone had stuck a knife through my heart. I was having trouble breathing. I tried to tell myself there had to be an innocent explanation even though I knew there wasn't. The man I loved had gone and married someone else behind my back. It was the worst thing he could have done.

Later, when I saw his car pull onto the forecourt, Nick at the wheel, his mate Jimmy West with him, I felt the pain in my chest start up again. Sue looked at me in alarm.

'You OK? You've gone white,' she said.

Nick came in and stood for a moment facing me. 'Jenny,' he said, coming over and getting hold of my hands. I wanted to yank them away and tell him what I thought of him but I couldn't seem to move or get a word out.

'I need you to know what's going on,' he said.

I found my voice. 'I *already* know! You just married someone else. Your *ex*. I *saw* you.' Tears welled up. He looked ready to cry as well. The sight of him in his wedding suit, too good-looking for words, twisted my insides. It was how I'd imagined him looking on our wedding day.

'Leave me alone,' I said, tears running down my face.

'It's all right,' he said. 'It's all right.'

It would never be all right, not after what he'd gone and done.

'Just listen for a minute, let me explain.' He still had hold of me.

I didn't want him to explain. I wouldn't look at him while he told me about Lisa being pregnant, claiming it was his baby when he knew full-well it wasn't. She had managed to convince his mum, he said, who had put pressure on him to do the decent thing.

'It's not mine, I swear.' He gave me a pleading look. 'Once it's born I'll get blood tests done and prove it.' He was a rare blood group, he said. It was the first I'd heard of it. 'I'll be able to get the marriage annulled.' He perked up. 'It'll be like it never happened.'

My heart was in pieces. It didn't matter what he said, the fact was he had gone and got married. Without a word to me. No blood tests or annulment, or anything else, was going to make a difference now.

When I got home Mum took one look at me and jumped up out of her chair. 'What's the matter?' she said. She led me to the sofa and sat me down. 'You're white as a sheet.' I looked at her, broken. 'Come on, tell me,' she said, giving me a cuddle.

I put my head in her lap and started sobbing. She held me and shushed me and waited for me to calm down and I stuttered and sobbed and told her about Nick getting married. She let me take my time and stroked my hair the way she used to when I was poorly in hospital. Eventually, she said, 'One day you'll thank your lucky stars he married someone else.'

It was years before I found out that the summer before, when Nick had come back from Yarmouth, he'd had his holiday snaps developed at the shop down the road from us and the woman who ran the place – knowing he was seeing me – let Mum know he was all over some girl in the photos. That week, when he'd phoned every night saying how much he loved me, that he missed me, he was with someone else. Lisa, it turned out. Sneaking off to phone me, lying to her. Lying to me. Liar. *Liar.* Poor Mum, seeing how happy I was with him, couldn't bring herself to say anything and kept hoping things would fizzle out of their own accord.

It explained why she'd gone off him all of a sudden.

For weeks I was in a dreadful state, walking round like a zombie. Not eating, not sleeping. I couldn't stop crying. The pain was unbearable. To make matters worse, Nick wouldn't leave me alone. Everywhere I went, there he was. He parked up outside the garage and waited for me to get off work. Hung around at the end of the road. I refused to have anything to do with him. He must have been desperate because he had the nerve to come to the house one day. Mum answered the door and chased him down the road.

'If you think I brought that girl into the world for the likes of you, you've got another thing coming,' she shouted after him.

It was as if my world had ended. All my dreams gone. Even though I knew he was no good for me the feelings I had for him wouldn't just go away. At my worst, I didn't see the point in carrying on. I really believed that nothing could ever make me feel as bad again.

I was wrong about that.

13.

I was coming up to my seventeenth birthday when Nick got in touch and asked if I'd have a drink with him.

'Just to celebrate our birthdays,' he said.

He wanted to explain. About Lisa. And the baby. The one that wasn't his.

'Just hear me out and if you still want nothing more to do with me, I'll leave you alone, I promise. That'll be the end of it,' he said.

I was feeling better by then. Over him. Sick of seeing him at every turn. One night in his company to get him off my back once and for all seemed a small price to pay. What harm could it do? Course, I knew Mum would hit the roof if she knew what I was planning so I kept quiet. She and Dad were going to be away that week anyway, at the caravan on Canvey Island. I thought they'd never find out. They might not have done either if I hadn't invited Nick in for a coffee when he dropped me off at the end of the night. We were sitting there when the phone went.

Patricia answered. It was Mum.

'Jenny's got Nick here,' she said, landing me straight in it.

Mum went mad and told Patricia to put me on. I wouldn't talk to her. I knew I was in for a rollicking. Patricia was shouting, telling me to get on the phone, calling me a little cow. I told Nick he'd better go.

'See what you've done?' Patricia slammed the phone back in its cradle. 'They're coming back early now, all because of you, you selfish cow.'

I felt awful. Mum was the one who'd picked me up off the floor when Nick broke my heart. And now, soon as her back was turned, I'd let him in again. Only it wasn't like that. I wasn't back with him at all. Even though I wasn't quite as over him as I liked to make out I felt strong, not about to let him string me along again. I'd learned a painful lesson and despite all his pleading for another chance I had told him to leave me alone and go back to his wife.

What I should have done was said all that to Mum because it was what she needed to hear to put her mind at rest. Instead, she must have thought Nick had talked me round, that I was setting myself up again for yet more heartache.

More than anything, I wished I had spoken to her that night when I had the chance.

I didn't sleep well, thinking of Mum and Dad in the caravan, cutting short their holiday because of me. By rights, I should have been with them, and I would have been if I'd not made plans with Nick. I wished I had gone. I loved it at Canvey. A memory came back from when I was little, of being at the seaside, my dad going off to work every morning and getting the train back at the end of the day. Me running along the sea wall to meet him from the station, being carried on his shoulders.

For hours I lay in the dark thinking about what I'd say to Mum when she got back. Once I told her I wasn't back with Nick it would be OK. I must have drifted off to sleep because I dreamed about Mum. It was the day Nick got married, only this time Mum was the one sobbing and I didn't know why. It was her head in my lap, me cuddling her. Her hair was long, like it used to be when I was little. I woke up with a start, tearful and out of sorts. The dream had unsettled me. It went through my mind again that I should have spoken to her night before.

Put things right when I had the chance.

14.

I'd always wanted black hair like my mum and for a couple of years I'd been colouring it. I liked it dark. Everyone thought it suited me, especially as my eyebrows were dark to start with. The day after Mum phoned from Canvey I was in the bathroom putting hair dye on when there was a knock at the front door. I shouted for Patricia to go and squeezed some dye out of the little applicator bottle, working it onto my fringe, trying not to let any of it drip in the sink. Another knock. Louder, this time. I listened for Patricia thumping down the stairs. Nothing. With my hair half-done I went to see who it was. Two policemen stood on the doorstep.

'Is your mum in?' the taller of the two said.

'She's away.'

'What about your dad?'

'They're on holiday.'

'What's their car registration?'

I told them. They looked at each other.

'Is there anyone else in the house?' This was the shorter

one.

'My big sister's in.'

'Can you go and get her?'

I ran upstairs and banged on the bedroom door. 'You need to come down,' I said.

Patricia appeared with a face like thunder.

'The police are here,' I said.

We had to go down to the station to clear something up, they said. I wanted to rinse the dye off my hair first but they wouldn't let me. We got in the back of the police car, me with my fringe full of hair dye, Patricia with her face tripping her up. The one who was driving, the tall one, took off his hat and gave it to me to hold for him. As we drove through Walthamstow it seemed as if everyone was looking at us. I couldn't think what could have happened for the police to send a car to the house.

At the station they put us in a bare little room with a table that wobbled and flimsy plastic seats that felt as if they'd break if you leaned too far back in them. The door had a small round window in it at eye level, like a porthole. We sat there for ages. Hours. Every now and then someone would peer in at us through the glass in the door.

'How long they going keep us sat here?' Patricia said, looking worried.

I didn't answer. The room was cold and I only had a thin top on. I folded my arms and hugged myself.

'What the bloody hell's going on? Why don't they just tell us something?' Patricia said.

'It'll be Mum,' I said. 'She's pranged the car, I bet.'

I lost all track of time as we waited in that little room with its rickety table. Eventually, four or five police officers crowded in and stood facing us. The one I took to be the most important, going on his age and the fancy ribbons on his uniform, said he had bad news.

He cleared his throat, looked from me to Patricia. 'There's been an accident,' he said. I knew it. 'We don't know exactly what happened yet.' He started saying it looked like Mum had been going down the road the wrong way and hit a petrol tanker. They were in Upminster, on the Southend Arterial, on their way from Canvey to Walthamstow, when the crash happened.

I looked at Patricia. She was frowning.

'Are they hurt?' I said.

He hesitated. 'The car went up in flames.'

'How bad was it?'

'About as bad as it can be,' he said.

It was my dad I thought about first. Ever since the thrombosis he had not been a well man. His heart wasn't good. Of the two of them, he was the one I thought of as frail, less likely to survive an accident.

I said, 'How's me dad?'

Silence, then, 'Your dad's dead.'

It went through my mind that Mum must be in a dreadful state. They were inseparable so how she'd get over losing him I couldn't imagine. Patricia still hadn't said anything. 'What about me mum?' I asked.

The policeman shook his head. Tears ran down his face. 'I'm sorry ...'

I jumped out of my seat and flew at him, beating my fists on his chest. 'No, no! You've got it wrong!'

Patricia was on her feet shouting as well. 'They shouldn't even have been coming home today! This is your fault! If you weren't such a selfish little cow they'd still be at the caravan!'

The policeman held onto me. I was hitting him, saying it was all lies, they'd got the wrong people. He kept saying how sorry he was while Patricia ranted in the background, calling me a bastard, saying they should never have been on the road in the first place.

They sat us back down and asked if there was anyone they could call. Patricia said Eddie, her fiancé. The only person I could think of was Nick Benson.

The police needed us to go to Upminster Station and identify some of the things recovered from Mum's and Dad's car. Nick drove us. We were led into another gloomy little room where a few items were laid out on the table: a towel covered in blood that was part of a set Mum had got down the market. Her handbag. The shoes they'd had on. Everything was charred. The air smelled of smoke.

I looked at their belongings. Was that all there was? When I asked to see my parents the police officers exchanged a look. 'You don't want to see them like this,' one said. I did, though. I stared at their burnt things, refusing to believe it was my mum and dad who'd been in the car. It had to be a mistake. I was desperate, saying I needed to see them, asking Nick to get them to take me. The policemen stood like sentries blocking the door. A tremor went through me and I started shaking uncontrollably. A woman police officer brought in a cup of tea and held it to my lips but I couldn't get it down. It was as if my throat had closed up.

Nick drove us round to my other sisters, one by one, to break the news. Patricia had to tell them because my voice had gone. I saw the looks on their faces, the shock as they registered what she was saying. No one could work out what Mum and Dad were doing coming home halfway through their holiday. Patricia put them straight. I was left in no doubt that what had happened was my fault.

I'd as good as killed them.

The next day Patricia went to stay with my sister Jean and I went to Lizzie's. I left a note on the door at home saying I was at such and such an address if anyone was looking for me. I still hadn't uttered a word since the day before at the police station when I'd asked to see Mum and Dad. Lizzie was getting worried. I don't know why but she thought it might make me feel better if I saw where the accident had happened. We went down there, drove past the black skid marks in the road, and ended up at the garage that had recovered my parents' car. It was brand new but all that remained was a scorched shell. A few scraps of leather upholstery clung to what was left of the front seats. I tried not to think of Mum behind the wheel, Dad beside her, the car in flames. A bit of blackened material was stuck to the base of the metal frame on the passenger seat. I reached inside the car. Lizzie told me to leave it, not to touch anything. I pulled at the material. It was a bit of the waistband of my dad's trousers and his pants. I think that was what tipped me over the edge and on the way home in the car I started screaming and couldn't stop. Lizzie pulled over and tried to calm me down but I was hysterical. Inconsolable. I sobbed and screamed and hung onto the bit of tattered material I'd rescued from the car.

That night Lisa, Nick's wife, turned up at Lizzie's looking for me. She must have been to Forest Road and seen the note on the door. She had a mate with her, a real loudmouth, shouting the odds. The pair of them started effing and blinding from the off, making enough commotion to bring the whole street out. Next door's curtains twitched. Lizzie came to see what all the noise was about.

'Do you know our parents were killed yesterday?' Lizzie said, glaring at them.

'And do *you* know she's trying to take her husband?' the friend said.

Lisa cut in. 'If you want him, come and get him.'

I snapped. 'I haven't got time. Just send him round.' It was the first thing I'd said for nearly two days.

They were still shouting and swearing when Lizzie shut the door on them.

15.

I went home after a couple of days. Patricia was still at Jean's so I had the place to myself. Seeing the burned-out car had sent me a bit mad. In spite everything, I had a hard time believing my parents had really gone. If they were dead how come no one would let me see them? I thought if I could sit with them for a minute, hold my mum's hand, it might sink in. It was no use asking. I kept getting told, 'No.' Even Nick trotted out what the police had said about it not helping to see them. It seemed everyone else thought they knew what was best, yet how could they? It was *my* mum and dad we were talking about.

I decided the two people in the mortuary were imposters and made up a story in my head about Mum and Dad being held prisoner somewhere. Every afternoon I made a pot of tea and put it on a tray with cups and saucers, took it into the living room, and waited for them to come in. I'd sit there, staring at the door, willing it to open, the tea going cold in the pot. If I kept on making tea for them, they were bound to come, was how I saw it. No one knew what I was doing. None of my sisters came near. I was glad about that. The only one who'd told me to my face I was to blame for what had happened was Patricia but in my grief I was convinced the rest of them thought the same.

Not a day went by without Nick coming round to see how I was. I didn't tell him about the tea business – or about Mum and Dad being held captive. I knew he wouldn't understand. No one would. Nick ironed my clothes, did beans on toast or a bowl of soup, and sat there while I picked at whatever he put in front of me. I didn't eat much. I had no appetite. The weight started falling off. Nick would give me a look and plead with me to eat something. There was no point making myself ill, he said. I didn't see why not.

I couldn't get past the guilt eating away at my insides.

All the talk was about post mortems and inquests and funeral arrangements. My sister, Gillian, heavily pregnant, was distraught. Everyone was, and it was down to me. I'd always got along with my sisters, except Patricia, but I sensed that everything had changed. I was tormented thinking about the night I'd brought Nick back and Mum ringing, me digging my heels in and refusing to speak to her. *If only.* I couldn't get away from the voice in my head that kept on at me, saying what a selfish cow I was and if it weren't for me Mum and Dad would still be here. It was sending me mad. I couldn't work so Mandy covered for me at the garage. At home, on my own, I started drinking. Vodka. Enough to blot it all out. If I went out I'd have a bottle hidden inside my jacket and slip into shop doorways for a sneaky swig. I couldn't get on a bus unless I had a bottle on me. Nick could see what I was doing. He had a go about the drink as well.

'It's not going to change anything,' he said.

He was wrong. It changed how bad I felt. For a while at least.

I'd go into my parents' bedroom and look at their things, stretch out on the bed with my head on Mum's pillow and imagine her and Dad coming back and being pleased because the place was exactly as they'd left it. Then the voice in my head would start up again. *They're not coming back.* I'd bury my face in the pillow but I couldn't make it stop. *They're never coming back.* On and on it went. In the end, I'd get up and go downstairs and drink myself stupid.

One thing I couldn't stand was to be in the house by myself overnight so one of my friends would come round. Babs from the garage, or Fat June, usually. I liked it when Fat June came because she talked non-stop and I didn't have to say anything. Fat June could have a conversation all by herself.

I was starting to like the drink, the woozy, fuzzy feel of it. Being drunk was a lot better than being sober. One night Nick called round and pleaded with me to get some food inside me. He watched me nibble half-heartedly on a bit of toast before giving up. Once he'd gone I ran a bath. Steam filled the room. I had a bit to drink while the water was running. In the bathroom cabinet were pills belonging to my dad. I looked at the little brown bottles with their printed labels made out to Mr Alfred Jones. He wasn't going to need them now. I lined them up on the edge of the bath next to the taps. The water was too hot but I got in anyway, not caring when it burned me. Even in my drunken state I could see how thin I'd got. Six stone something, skin and bone. All my ribs were showing and my legs were like little sticks. I sat with my knees poking up out of the water, knocking back vodka from the bottle, aching for my mum. As the bath went cold I kept on drinking, waiting for the booze to send me into oblivion, all the while eyeing up my dad's pills. I took the lid off one of the bottles and tipped some into my hand. Little white capsules. I swallowed them. Washed them down with the vodka. Took the rest. Started on the next bottle. I didn't stop until I'd taken the lot and finished the last of the booze.

It was Nick who found me.

Earlier in the evening he'd thought there was something different about me – that I was more out of it than usual. I had a look in my eyes, he said, that played on his mind, enough for him to come back after a few hours to check that I was alright. When I didn't answer the door he looked through the letterbox and saw me on the floor in the hall. I'd given him a key for emergencies and seconds later he was on his knees beside me, shaking me, trying to get me to wake up. When he couldn't bring me round he picked me up, ran out to the car, and sped to the nearest A & E. I was drifting in and out of consciousness when he carried me into the emergency department where they pumped my stomach. When I woke up I was like a wild thing, shouting and swearing and trying to get out of bed. I kept pulling the drip out the back of my hand, making such a mess they had to put stitches in. Every time anyone came near I lashed out at them. My language was terrible. In between the abuse I begged them to let me die. The doctor who treated me told me all this the next day when I was sitting up in bed, sober.

He asked what was behind the previous night's episode and I told him about my parents, about the voice in my head, and how all I could see in front of me was nothingness. He nodded and made notes and waited for me to finish.

'What you did last night was a determined attempt to take your life,' he said, eventually. 'You're lucky to be here.' Was I? 'You need help, Jenny.'

'I'm fine now,' I said.

He gave me a long look. 'I'm going to be blunt. If we let you walk out of this hospital I don't think you'll last the week. You need proper treatment.'

What he meant by that was round the clock medical supervision in what he called a place of safety.

'For as long as is necessary,' he said.

It was Clayberry Hospital he wanted to send me to, the mental institution. I was horrified. I told him I wanted to go home.

'In my opinion, you shouldn't be living on your own. It's not safe. You're seventeen, not in a position to discharge yourself – and I'm certainly not about to discharge you.' He looked at me, solemn and concerned. 'Think about what I've said.'

I lay there, frightened. If I ended up in Clayberry who knew when I might get out? It was something that would be with me for the rest of my life. The thought made me frantic. I called Lizzie and told her what had happened.

'You've brought it on yourself,' she said, furious.

'I need you to come and discharge me or they'll send me away.' I was desperate. 'Please.'

The line went quiet. Lizzie sighed. 'It might be best if you did go into Clayberry. Just for a bit. Until you get yourself sorted out.'

I hung onto the phone, feeling cold and clammy and panicky. 'If you let me go in there I'll never forgive you. It'll be a stigma for the rest of my life, I can't end up-'

Lizzie cut in. 'Oh, you bloody little cow, do what you want. You think I haven't got enough going on without all this? It's hard for all of us, you know, without you making things worse.'

When she came in and signed the papers to have me discharged she was in a foul mood. She looked at me, still in my hospital gown, my hand bandaged where the drip had been. 'That's it. I wash my hands of you. You can please yourself from now on,' she said.

With that she turned and went.

I had no money so I got dressed and walked home.

I was grateful to Nick. He had saved my life. I knew how worried about me he was. After what had happened he didn't want to let me out of his sight and spent as much time as he could at the house. It didn't change the pain I felt over his marrying Lisa, but I did begin to mellow. He couldn't have been kinder, fussing over me, there whenever I needed him. I was still wary but at the same time I knew I'd never stopped loving him.

It was weeks before we could have the funeral. Post mortems had to be done and they held things up. It all seemed to drag on endlessly and meanwhile I was all over the place, up and down, drinking and crying, and never very far from the edge of utter despair.

Nick kept me going.

Without him and a few good friends propping me up, I'm pretty sure I'd have gone under.

The funeral was at the City of London Crematorium. I don't remember much about it, just the two hearses filled with flowers pulling up, and seeing my sisters reflected in the long side windows of the funeral cars, crying. I wanted to say there was no need to get upset because the people in those coffins weren't Mum and Dad. The only way I could get through the day was by pretending it was all a mistake. Making up a story in my head.

Lots of people came to the cemetery to pay their respects, including a couple of friends of my dad's, who flew over from America. I did a double-take at the sight of a man who looked exactly like my dad, only shorter. It turned out to be his brother. None of us had seen him before. Everyone came back to the house in Forest Road where I'd laid on sandwiches and was in and out of the kitchen making endless pots of tea. I wanted to keep busy. Didn't want to stop and think about what was really happening and why the house was full of chat and laughter.

Once we'd got the funeral over, I went back to work at the garage. I thought about my parents constantly. Dreamed about them – horrible upsetting dreams where Mum was crying and I couldn't do a thing to make her feel better. I would wake up in tears, covered in sweat.

We still didn't know what had happened on the day of the accident, although what the police had said about Mum driving the wrong way down the road wasn't right. There was no petrol tanker either, that much we knew. We were going to have to wait until the inquest to get to the bottom of things. In the meantime, it was hard not to speculate. Nick was round my place all the time. Someone he knew who'd been on the same road at the same time, going the same way as Mum and Dad, told him he'd seen a van fly past shortly before the crash.

'He's going to kill someone going at that speed,' he'd said to his passenger, as the van tore off up the road.

A bit further on he came across the accident. Mum and Dad's car in flames with them in it, the same van smashed up and, at the side of the road, the bloke who'd been driving it, not a scratch on him, moaning about writing it off.

I wanted to go and find him and kill him.

'It'll come out at the inquest,' Nick said. According to him, the van guy worked for a company everyone had heard of. 'He won't get away with it, don't worry.'

Everything seemed to hinge on the inquest. Mum's and Dad's car insurance wouldn't pay out, saying they had questions about my dad's health and wanted to wait until after the coroner had delivered a verdict. It became obvious what they were getting at, that somehow Dad had suffered a heart attack and collapsed onto my mum causing her to swerve and crash. I felt like screaming. Again, Nick told me not to worry. The inquest would sort things once and for all.

There was nothing to do but wait.

The day before the inquest opened in Romford I was at the

front of the house watering the geranium my mum had been growing in a pot. The plant was lovely, doing really well. I was standing admiring it when a woman I didn't know stopped and asked if she could have it.

I was taken aback. 'No, you can't,' I said.

'Your mum promised it to me.'

I knew that couldn't be right. 'Why would she do that?'

'She just did. She knew I liked it. You'll only let it die.'

'I don't care, you're not having it.'

She stood for a while longer before heading off down the road. One of the neighbours coming the other way must have seen the look on my face because she stopped to have a word.

'You all right, Jenny? Your mum's geranium's looking lovely.' For a horrible moment I thought she was about to ask if *she* could have it. 'You know, you were the apple of your mum's eye,' she said. 'Your dad's as well. Don't let anyone tell you any different.'

I looked away, embarrassed. Didn't she know it was me who'd killed them?

I had no idea what to expect from the inquest, never having been to one. I pictured a kindly coroner determined to make the process as painless as possible for us, the family. In my mind's eye I saw the van driver stand up and admit the accident was his fault. The police would come and cart him off. I dared to entertain the thought that people might stop blaming me. Maybe in time, I might even stop blaming myself.

That was how naïve I was.

The coroner turned out to be bad-tempered and irritable, the fact he was dealing with a bereaved family seemingly neither here nor there to him. He frowned and scowled and grumbled under his breath.

'I don't want any outbursts from the family – aunts, uncles, children …' he said, glaring at us, as he opened the proceedings.

Not a good start.

The bloke who'd been driving the van was tall and thin with greasy hair and a face that was all sharp angles. He came into court with an exaggerated limp, hobbling along as if every step was agony. When he gave his evidence he didn't say anything like what I was expecting. My mum had swerved, he said, and he couldn't avoid hitting her. I waited for the coroner to pull him up, challenge him, but all he did was nod and write stuff down.

'How fast were you going?' the coroner asked, still writing on his pad, not looking up.

'At least forty.'

The coroner made a note. I felt sure he would have something to say about that. *At least forty* could mean anything. When nothing was said I wanted to jump up and say he'd been speeding, doing more like eighty than forty, from what I'd heard.

Another witness, who had stopped to help, described how he had been beaten back by the intense heat and flames. The car was well alight, my parents trapped inside, my mother screaming. The poor man was close to tears giving his evidence. 'I couldn't get near,' he said, his voice breaking.

I put my hands over my ears wishing I hadn't come while the coroner frowned and scribbled away on his pad.

In the end, no one blamed the van driver.

It was *one of those things*.

A terrible tragedy.

An accident.

An open verdict was recorded.

Afterwards, we went to the pub over the road and my brother put Mum's jewellery on the table. It didn't amount to much: two gold lockets – one I'd had made for her, dotted with tiny rubies – earrings, a watch, the bangle she'd had on when she died. Her diamond rings. The others helped themselves. The bangle, charred from the fire, was left on the table. Mum had always said the rings were for Patricia and me. Patricia took hers while Jean made a grab for the other one.

Patricia piped up. 'Mum said that was for Jenny.'

'I don't think she's in any fit state to have it just yet,' Jean said, putting it on. It was a lovely ring, a rectangular setting studded with stones. 'I'll look after it until she feels better.' She pushed the bangle towards me. 'Tell you what, you have that, Jenny.'

I never did get the ring.

When I got home the geranium at the front of the house had gone.

16.

Months after the accident I was still in a bad way, grieving for my mum and dad. Every day I went to the cemetery to visit the grave where their remains were buried. I would sit on the grass, sometimes for hours. My friend Babs tried to talk me out of going. One day she dropped me at the gates and offered to come in with me but I wouldn't let her.

'You going in there by yourself was one of the saddest things I've ever seen,' she said the next day. 'You looked so lost and lonely it broke my heart. Let me come with you, eh?'

It was good of her but I didn't want the company.

It didn't matter what the weather was doing, I still went to the cemetery. One day it was pouring with rain and I was sitting on the sodden earth in a little light-coloured suit and a pair of beige suede boots, wet through, when a voice said, 'Don't cry.'

I looked up to see a man a few feet away in grey flannels and a short-sleeved shirt, no jacket. He was bone dry.

'You wouldn't want them back, not the way they were.'

What did he know? 'I would.' I was crying harder now.

'Not like that you wouldn't.' He had a nice voice, kind. 'Come on, dry your eyes.'

Water had seeped through my boots and my feet were sopping. My hair was plastered to my scalp. I wondered how come he wasn't wet and was about to ask but when I looked up he was gone. I scrambled to my feet and gazed all around. Nowhere in sight. I'd only taken my eyes off him for a second or two, not long enough for him to have vanished into thin air. I stayed at the grave a bit longer, thinking about what he'd said about not wanting my parents back *the way they were*, wondering who he was and how he knew. From then on, every day when I went to the cemetery I was on the lookout for him but I never saw him again.

By now, Nick had left Lisa and was living with me. He wouldn't say what had gone on between them in the end, just that he would never have married her if she hadn't been pregnant. I noticed he'd gone quiet on the subject of the baby not being his and getting blood tests done to prove it. I didn't bring up the matter of his rare blood type and neither did he.

Not long after the accident, Patricia and Eddie got married. She asked if they could move in with me for a bit until they got on their feet. I said no. We'd ever got on and things were even worse between us now. My eldest sister Jean got on the phone and let rip.

'I can't believe you won't let them stay with you,' she said. 'It's only for a couple of weeks. You'd see your own sister without a roof over her head, you little cow.'

I thought about it. Two weeks. If that was all it was going to be it wouldn't be too bad. I said OK, they could move in.

After two weeks they showed no sign of moving out. The weeks became months. A washing machine appeared in the kitchen. I asked Patricia how much longer they were staying. She said it was taking longer than they had thought to get things sorted.

One day I got a call from a woman at the council to say Patricia had been to the housing department to ask if they could move me into a bedsit so that she and Eddie could take over the tenancy on the house.

'I thought you should know,' the woman said. 'With a sister like that you certainly don't need enemies.'

By now, Patricia was pregnant. 'You'd chuck me out when I'm expecting a baby?' she said, when I confronted her.

I couldn't believe the cheek of her. 'You're the one going behind my back trying to chuck *me* out!'

The atmosphere was awful.

At least I had Nick. I really thought we would be OK. He had seen me at my worst, at rock bottom, and was still there at every turn, stopping me from going under. I was so in love, more than ever.

He was my world.

One day there was a knock at the door and when I opened it there was Lisa with her baby. The last time I'd seen her was at Lizzie's the day after my parents were killed and she was on the warpath. At least this time she seemed to be in a better mood.

'I don't want trouble,' she said. 'Just a chat. About Nick.'

I asked her in.

'You know he's been seeing me?' she said. 'Coming round, spending the night?'

I didn't. He'd been working away, as far as I knew.

Lisa said the way he was flitting in and out of her life was driving her mad. 'I can't have it,' she said. 'Not with the baby to think about.'

I made some tea but couldn't get it down. My stomach was churning. I was seventeen years old. Only a few months had gone by since my parents had died. I didn't know how to deal with any of this.

'Look, I'm sorry about coming round shouting the odds that night at your sister's,' Lisa said. 'He did say your parents had been killed but I didn't believe him. I thought it was another of his lies.'

I sat, dazed, trying to take it in.

She gave a shrug. 'I'm sick of it. He needs to make up his mind – then we can all get on with things.'

We waited for him to come in from work. My head was spinning.

'Maybe you and me should share a place,' Lisa said, making me smile. 'He couldn't mess us about then, could he?'

When Nick came in and saw Lisa sitting there his face was a picture.

He hovered for a minute inside the doorway and I had the feeling he might turn round and go straight back out again. In the end, he came in and sat in a chair facing us. 'Don't suppose there's any tea going?' he said, casual as you like.

Lisa did most of the talking. There was no shouting, no

tears. All she did was put her foot down and tell him he had to decide once and for all who he wanted to be with. My heart was like a stone inside my chest. I already knew what he would say. Lisa was his wife, after all. She had his baby. Sitting there, waiting for him to make up his mind, I had a sudden sense it would be best for me if he chose her. It was all too complicated, too fraught. I didn't want any of this. He shot me a look. I kept quiet. No one said anything for what seemed like an age.

'Jenny,' he said at last. 'That's who I want.'

My jaw dropped. It was the last thing I expected to hear.

Lisa stayed silent. After a few seconds she got to her feet. The baby was sleeping, his face pressed against her. She nodded at me. 'Thanks for the tea,' she said, hoisting her bag over a shoulder. 'You know, if things were different I think you and me could have been friends.'

Nick waited for her to go and smiled, awkward. 'It wasn't like I was sleeping with her or anything,' he said. 'I was only going round to see she was all right, her and the baby. I swear that's all it was.'

I didn't know what to think.

'Say something,' he said, coming over and getting hold of my hand. 'I should have said about Lisa but I didn't want you getting the wrong idea, thinking something was going on when it wasn't. You've been in such a bad way. I was only trying to look out for you.' He stroked my wrist. 'Look, I'll get the divorce sorted and we'll get married. You know how I feel about you.'

I looked into his eyes. Blue, like the sea. I loved him and at the same time knew he was no good for me. My feelings were all over the place. I was torn between wishing he would go and wanting to be with him. 'You'd better get after her, take her home, at least,' I said. 'You can't leave her to get the bus with the baby.'

He went looking for her but it was too late.

She had already gone.

17.

I couldn't stop thinking about my parents. I kept having the same bad dream – me at the side of the road, rooted to the spot, the car in flames. The heat was unbearable, the air thick with choking smoke. Mum and Dad trapped while I stood by, helpless. I'd wake in tears, sweat pouring off me, and lie for hours in the dark, everything I'd heard at the inquest going round and round in my head, convinced them dying was my fault. The thought haunted me. I kept thinking about Mum phoning that night from Canvey. As time went on, the guilt got worse. It got so I really didn't like myself. The mean little voice inside my head told me I was a bad person, a selfish little cow; that I deserved to suffer.

I was still working at the garage, going in some days with my nerves jangling, after almost no sleep. What with the tiredness, the guilt and endless self-recrimination, I was in no mood to take any nonsense from anyone. There was a girl I worked with, Angie, who was gay and had a thing about me. She was forever saying she fancied me, even though she already had a girlfriend and knew I was with Nick. All the time, she pushed and pushed, wanting a reaction. To start with I tried to make light of it but she wouldn't let up and pestered the life out of me. If any of the blokes who came in for petrol stopped for a chat and I was friendly back she'd call me all sorts of horrible names. It had been going on a while. One night, at the end of my shift when I was about to go home she got hold of my bag and threw it across the floor. All my stuff tipped out. I had to get on my hands and knees and scrabble about while she sneered and called me a few choice names. I'd only just picked everything up when she grabbed the bag off me and upended it again. The clasp on my purse came undone and money went skittering in every direction. It was the final straw. As I picked up the last of my things something inside me snapped and before I knew what I was doing I'd smacked her in the face. She put a hand up to her eye. I was as shocked as she was. For a few seconds she stared at me, open-mouthed.

'What have you done, you mad cow?' she said, at last.

I was shaking. 'From now on, leave me alone.'

The next day when I got to work everyone was talking about what had happened the night before, me landing Angie one. She had a dreadful black eye, apparently, a real shiner.

I braced myself, thinking I was in serious trouble. I'd get the sack. The police would be round. There was bound to be some kind of fallout. I needn't have worried. According to Sue, Angie was wearing her injury like a badge of honour, telling anyone willing to listen I'd flown at her in a fit of passion.

'You should hear her,' Sue said. '*Bragging. Proud.* Saying you'd never have gone for her if you weren't interested. She reckons it's proof you fancy her, deep down …'

I couldn't think of anything to say to that.

A year after losing my parents I discovered I was pregnant. It was the best thing that could have happened. I felt I'd been given a chance to start again, create a new family of my own. The baby was all I wanted. When I told Nick the news he was delighted.

'I'll look after you,' he said, putting a hand on my belly, even though I was only a few weeks gone and there was no sign of a bump.

Patricia and Eddie were still living with us. She was pregnant as well, the baby due in a few weeks. I couldn't see them moving out any time soon.

I was a few months into the pregnancy when Nick didn't come home one night. It was almost midnight when the police phoned to say he'd been arrested and was being held overnight at Stratford before appearing in court the next morning. The police officer who rang said he wasn't sure what he'd done, only that it was to do with a theft from the garage where he worked. It turned out Nick and another bloke had been helping themselves to tyres and selling them on the side. The magistrate remanded him in custody to Brixton Prison. A couple of days later I went to visit him.

He faced me across a table with a glass partition separating us.

'They've got it wrong,' he said, looking put out. 'It was nothing to do with me.'

I looked at him. Unshaven, rumpled, as if he'd slept in his

clothes and hadn't put a comb through his hair. Killer blue eyes on me. Even in his scruffy state he managed to do funny things to my insides. I put a protective hand on my bump. He was talking about some other bloke at work, 'a bad lot,' who'd been nicking stuff for ages, and was the real culprit. He'd been picked up too.

'I reckon he must have dropped me in it,' he said.

It was hard to concentrate because the woman next to me was having a right go at the bloke she was visiting, saying that was it, she'd had enough. I couldn't hear his side of things, just her, shaking her head, going, 'Liar. You think I was born yesterday?'

Nick said, 'Jenny, I swear, it's nothing to do with me.'

I made a few more visits to Brixton, a part of London I didn't know. It felt noisy and crowded and alien. Walking up Brixton Hill one day, a man with wild eyes and a dirty old coat blocked my way and asked if I loved Jesus. I tried to get past but he came with me talking about repentance and God loving sinners. I kept my eyes down and hurried along, shaken, feeling as if the guilt I carried inside about my parents was visible to everyone.

At the prison, I'd wait with the other visitors, one of the staff patting me down and going through my bag before waving me through to a waiting area that was cold and bare and depressing. I never saw the woman again who was next to me that first time, the one who kept calling her bloke a liar.

Nick wasn't fazed by being in prison, going on about how he hadn't done anything and it was all a big mistake. He got friendly with the bloke he shared his cell with, a stocky lump with dead eyes who'd gone after his ex-girlfriend with a machete.

'They're back together again so he'll get off,' Nick said, as if I was interested in a man I didn't know who was locked up for a violent assault on his other half.

After two weeks on remand Nick was released pending his court case. Once he came out he changed his tune and stopped saying he was innocent. When I asked him what he'd been thinking, stealing stuff from work, he took his time answering.

'I was trying to earn extra money for the baby,' he said, eventually.

I stared at him.

'You being pregnant … I mean, we'll never get by on what's coming in. Not when you're not earning.' He looked at me, let it sink in. 'And when you think of all the stuff we're going to need …' A shrug. Helpless. 'It's on me, isn't it, all of it?'

I was knocked for six. It wasn't as if my being pregnant was an accident or unplanned. I had never made a secret of wanting a family of my own, and he had been as keen as I was. So he said, anyway. We had talked about the money side of things and how we'd manage with one wage coming in and I was in no doubt that when it came to it we'd be alright.

His words wormed their way inside my head. I had the feeling that everything I touched went bad, that I had no right to happiness. What everyone said about me being a little cow, a selfish one at that, was true.

It was why my parents were dead.

It was why Nick was in trouble with the law.

18.

I had a really bad time with the pregnancy. I had kidney infections, one after another, and was so sick. Not just the morning sickness that everyone told me would pass after the first few weeks but a nausea that came and went and had me throwing up all the way through. Some days I couldn't face food. Others, all I wanted was a piece of dry toast. I'd always loved sweets and chocolate but for the first time in my life I couldn't stomach them. None of it mattered. I was having my baby and that was all I cared about. Somehow, I knew all along I was having a girl and bought everything in pink. I kept working at the garage, steering clear of Angie. Once she realized I was pregnant she left me alone. Or it might have been because I'd slapped her.

Since his arrest, Nick seemed harder, more distant. I didn't know what he was doing or where he was half the time. When we went to see his solicitor ahead of the court case we were told there was every chance Nick would get a custodial sentence. I told myself the threat of prison hanging over him must be getting to him.

Sometimes he would call in at the garage when I was working. One night he brought a few beers and was leaning against the wall with a full pint glass in his hand. I was messing about, laughing about something – I don't even know what it was – when he flipped, no warning, and hurled his pint at me. I was soaked from head to toe.

I stared at him, beer running down my face, utterly shocked. He glared back at me. Babs, who was working that night, put a hand on my arm. Nick slammed his glass down and stormed out, banging the door behind him.

'What was that about?' Babs said, her face pale.

I shook my head. I had no idea. I tried to think what it was I'd said in the split second before he lashed out but my mind was blank.

Babs put an arm round me. 'You're white as a sheet. Are you all right?'

I wasn't sure. My legs felt ready to give way so I flopped into a chair.

'Has he done it before?' Babs was saying.

I shook my head. The look on his face, the fury that had come from nowhere, the sound of his car starting up and screeching away, made me feel sick. Babs made a cup of tea and stirred sugar into it, saying it was the best thing when you'd had a shock. I was shaking so hard I didn't dare take it from her in case I spilled it so she held it to my lips, making me think of the policewoman who'd done the same thing when we went to identify Mum's and Dad's things after the accident. All of a sudden I was in tears.

'Don't get upset.' Babs put the tea down and wiped my face as tears streamed down my cheeks. 'Here, don't cry. Come on, Jenny, you've got that baby to think about now.'

When I got home Nick was waiting, full of apologies. He didn't know what had come over him. He would never hurt me. Not in a million years. He felt terrible.

'I don't know how you can stand to look at me,' he said.

We sat on the bed, side by side, while he held my hand and promised it would never happen again.

'I love you,' he said, over and over.

I let him talk, my hair still wet and sticky from the beer, my clothes smelly. It wasn't very long before he was on about the court case and the baby and worrying about making ends meet.

'I've got a lot on my plate.' He stroked my damp hair. 'What with you and the baby and everything.'

I'd guessed as much. It was as if I'd been waiting for him to get to the point all along. The mean little voice inside my head piped up. *Look what he's done for you since your parents died. It's not him, it's you.* It was the sort of thing I'd been hearing all my life.

'We'll forget about it,' Nick was saying.

I hardly noticed when he got up and went to run me a bath.

By the time Patricia had her baby, a boy, she and Eddie had been in the house for a year. Once the baby came along the washing machine was going all the time. They'd bought electric heaters for upstairs and when they first brought them in it went through my head they'd cost a bit to run. I was braced for a big bill. It dropped through the letterbox with perfect timing just before Christmas and was way more than usual. I went to Patricia and said she'd have to cough up the bulk of it.

'We'll split it in half,' she said.

'Have you seen how much it is? You're the one who's run it up. I'm, not paying for your washer and heaters going the whole time.'

She called me a mean little cow, said I'd soon find out what it was like having a baby.

'Don't expect any help from me,' she said.

'Are you paying for what you've used or what?' I said.

'I'll do what's fair. Give you half.'

I snapped. 'You shouldn't even be here! You were only supposed to be coming for a fortnight – that was a year ago!'

I thought about what it was like having them live with us. Sitting at the table having dinner with Nick while Patricia and Eddie marched through to the kitchen, trailing their friends with them. We'd had endless rows about the phone, which was in the front room, our bedroom. Patricia thought nothing of barging in to make a call after we'd gone to bed. Plonking her fat behind down beside us as if we weren't there.

'I want you out,' I said.

Patricia scoffed. 'You can think again.'

An idea came to me. 'I'll get the locks changed if I have to. I mean it.'

A week later I came home from work and the first thing I saw when I opened the front door was that the stair carpet had gone. All up the walls were deep gouge marks. I stood for a minute, still with my key in the lock, baffled. I knew we'd not been burgled. No one would break in and steal the stair carpet. The house was silent, nobody home, no sound of the radio on upstairs or the baby crying. For once, even the washer wasn't going. I tiptoed up the stairs, stepping over bits of torn underlay, and pushed open the door to the room Patricia and Eddie had. It was empty. Not a stick of furniture. Curtains gone. Carpet taken up, just the tatty bit of felt that was underneath left behind. A foul stench hung in the air. I held my nose and went inside, inspecting the damage. There were dirty nappies in the corner, faeces smeared on the walls, wet patches on the floor. Great long track marks had been gouged out of the plaster. Empty milk cartons were strewn about, giving off a sour odour that turned my stomach. I guessed they explained the wet patches. I studied the ruined walls. On the one facing the window, written in what looked like excrement, was SELFISH LITTLE COW. I backed away and shut the door.

Patricia and Eddie had taken my furniture and gone, without a word, causing as much devastation in the process as they could.

I never spoke to my sister again.

19.

Around seven months into my pregnancy my blood pressure went through the roof. I was suffering from pre-eclampsia. The midwife was blunt. It was a serious condition, she said, and could prove fatal. She wanted me to go into Thorpe Coombe maternity hospital, in Walthamstow, and stay there until I had the baby. I said no. I didn't dare leave Nick, who had taken to going out all hours, never saying where he was, telling me it was to do with work. I wanted to know what kind of work he was doing in the middle of the night. I dug my heels in and, reluctantly, the midwife agreed to monitor my blood pressure at home, on condition I rested up. I did what I could but my blood pressure stayed at a dangerously high level.

On January 14, I went into labour. At Thorpe Coombe they did an X-ray and said the baby was overdue. They wanted to induce me but there were complications that meant they couldn't. It seemed the baby did not want to come. I was in labour for more than fifty hours, in agony for most of them. I had never experienced such pain. Every time I thought it couldn't get any worse it did. I was almost delirious and told the midwife I was ready to throw myself out of the window.

'All right, dear,' she said, 'but I don't think it'll help. You're on the ground floor …'

At 2.30 pm on January 16, I was being wheeled into the operating theatre, dosed up on Pethidine, for an emergency Caesarean, when the baby decided to come. In the end, it all happened in a rush and before I knew it my baby was in my arms. A beautiful girl, 6lb 7oz. So pretty, with dark auburn hair. She was perfect. I held her, laughing and crying at the same time. I already knew what I was going to call her: Michele.

After such a long and difficult labour they knocked me out to give me some rest before taking me back to the ward. When I came round, a familiar voice was saying my name. In the next bed was my mate, Pearl, from ante-natal classes.

It was such a lovely surprise seeing her I jumped up and did a little dance.

Pearl watched, amused, while I skipped about in a pair of bright yellow baby doll pyjamas. 'Tell you what, I'll have some of whatever you're having,' she said.

It wasn't the Pethidine making me giddy, I knew that. The joy I felt was down to my beautiful baby girl.

'What's happened to your bump?' Pearl said, frowning at my stomach.

I glanced down. My tummy was flat. I hadn't put on much weight while I was pregnant, about nine pounds, but by the look of things every bit of it had gone.

'That's what fifty hours in labour does for you,' I said,

delighted.

Pearl laughed. 'Sends you a bit doolally as well, by the look of things.'

I had never felt such overwhelming happiness. When I looked at Michele I felt complete. Right then, she was all that mattered. Nick arrived with a bouquet of sweet-smelling freesias. The fragrance filled the ward. Ever since, the scent of freesias has brought memories flooding back of having Michele and the all-consuming sense of joy I felt those first few days after she was born. I no longer cared where Nick was going or what he was doing. I wasn't in the least bit anxious about his looming court case. If he went to jail it would be alright. I had Michele.

I could cope with anything life threw at me.

Michele was only a few months old when Nick's court case came up. The solicitor was still warning us to expect a prison term. He seemed to think it would help if I went along as moral support.

'It won't do any harm for the court to see he's in a relationship and has a child,' the solicitor said. 'Besides, the magistrate likes a pretty face.'

I was already thinking about what I'd do if he was sent down. I wasn't worried. I knew I would manage. One day at a time. As it turned out I didn't have to because to everyone's surprise Nick got a suspended sentence.

'My lucky charm,' he said afterwards, throwing his arms around me, delighted.

Things settled down again and Nick started doing up the

house. He worked hard, making good the damage done to the upstairs and staircase by Patricia and Eddie, redecorating from top to bottom. In the living room, he opened up the fireplace and put in an oak mantelpiece, with exposed brick on the chimney breast. The way he did it, he managed to make it look as if it had been part of the house all along. We were happy, making a home together, bringing up our daughter.

Michele was about a year old and I was in bed waiting for Nick one night when I heard him go out. I went to the window and there he was, in his suit, getting into the car and driving off. It was late and he hadn't said a word about going anywhere. Hours went by. I started to think something bad must have happened, an accident. Every time a car came down the street I jumped out of bed. He was gone all night and by morning I was frantic. When he showed up he acted like I was making a fuss about nothing.

'Out,' he said, when I asked where he'd been.

'You've been gone all night. I was worried sick.'

He gave me a sharp look. 'I needed to get away for a bit, that's all.'

Away from what? He shrugged, wouldn't say.

'Why didn't you just tell me you were off out?'

He was getting impatient. 'Just leave it, will you? On and on and on! For Christ's sake, can't you just let it go!'

I caught a flicker of anger in his eyes. The same look I'd seen the night he'd chucked his drink over me.

'All I'm saying is you could have told me, saved me worrying,' I said.

'Stop nagging, will you! No wonder I didn't come home.'

He tapped the side of his head. 'I've had it up to here. Just *drop* it. You're really winding me up now.'

He changed out of his suit, put his work clothes on, and stomped off without saying goodbye.

I couldn't work out what had made him turn like that. What he'd said about me winding him up gnawed away at me. It went through my head that whenever something bad happened it was because of something I'd done. That was how it seemed to me. *I've had it up to here*. What was that supposed to mean? As far as I knew, we were doing all right. It was only the night before we'd been talking about putting a conservatory on the back of the house and knocking through the wall between the bathroom and toilet. I raked over the conversation again. Was it me, pushing him, expecting too much? Too wrapped up in Michele to notice he wasn't as keen as me? No. He was the one wanting to work on the house, get it looking nice. *We're a family now*, he'd said.

A week or so after all that an official-looking envelope came through the door. It was a parking fine for somewhere in Southend. When I looked at the date it was for the night he'd gone out and not come back. The paperwork said he was 'accompanied.' I asked who he was with and he said his mate, Jimmy West. I went round to see Jimmy, Michele in my arms, to find out what he thought he was playing at staying out all night with Nick when I was at home with a baby.

'I don't know what he's told you, Jenny, but I wasn't in Southend with him.'

The pair of them were close, always had been. It was Jimmy who was best man when Nick married Lisa.

'I'm not going to lie, he was there, but it wasn't with me,' Jimmy said. He looked at me, holding Michele. 'He was with some woman.'

I felt as if I'd been punched. 'He told me it was you,' I said.

'Well, he's lying.' His wife had come into the hall to see what was going on. 'Get rid of him,' Jimmy said. 'We'll look after the baby while you get on your feet and find someone worth having.'

In the background, his wife was nodding.

I stood there for a minute or two, feeling sick, what he'd said sinking in; that Nick was cheating on me. I went home determined to have it out with him.

He was in the kitchen buttering a couple of slices of bread, getting ham out of the fridge, making a sandwich, not looking at me as I told him what Jimmy had said.

'I don't believe it,' he said, not a bit worried. 'He's having you on.' He bit into the sandwich, chewed for a minute, looked thoughtful. 'Bet he doesn't want his missus knowing where he was.' Another bite of the sandwich. 'That's what's going on there.'

He stopped eating and came over, put his hands on my shoulders. 'I love you,' he said. 'You know that, don't you?'

I gazed up at him, brushed a crumb off his chin, not knowing what to think. We had a beautiful little girl. We were making a home together. I knew he was unreliable and at times I wasn't sure I could trust him. Yet, difficult as he was, he was deep under my skin and I loved him. He held me close and I wondered for the umpteenth time what someone like him saw in me, selfish little cow that I was. Thinking back, it shows how low my self-worth must have been, although at the time I didn't realise. I thought *I* was the problem, not him. As I searched his eyes for the truth, he smiled that lovely smile of his, giving me a look that let me know I was being silly, making a fuss about nothing. For the sake of keeping the peace, I let the Southend business go, not realizing it was only the beginning.

There was much worse to come.

20.

'Let's get married, make it official,' Nick said. Michele had just turned two and his divorce from Lisa had come through.

I wasn't sure. When I thought about marrying him what came to mind was the memory of him sailing past the garage that day with Lisa, ribbons on his car. 'We don't have to,' I said.

There was no putting him off. 'I want you to be my wife,' he said. 'It's what I've always wanted.'

We set the date for June 8, a Friday, the week before my twenty-first birthday. I was carried along by Nick's enthusiasm and invited everyone apart from Patricia. One by one, they all said they couldn't make it.

'If it had been a Saturday, you'd have been alright,' Jean said. 'Friday's a bad day.'

When I offered to arrange a reception for later on, once we'd been on honeymoon, suggesting we make it a Saturday, thinking that would be better for everyone, Jean said, 'Saturday's tricky. Any other day ...'

As the date got closer, it dawned on me that not a single member of my family would be at my wedding. I couldn't help thinking it had only been my mum and dad keeping us all together.

I wanted a traditional church ceremony at St John's, in Walthamstow. It wasn't as if I was a regular churchgoer but I liked it there. It was peaceful, somewhere to go when I wanted a bit of quiet time. Since I'd had Michele I wasn't going to the cemetery any more but I never stopped thinking about Mum and Dad. I'd go to St John's where I usually had the place to myself and could sit in peace for as long as I needed. It was a lovely old building with big stone arches and a high ceiling. Somehow, being there made me feel closer to my parents.

I had mixed feelings about the wedding. When I'd first got together with Nick and we talked about it I had visions of my dad walking me down the aisle, Mum all dressed up, looking proud, shedding a few tears. I pictured Nick at the altar in his suit, so handsome I'd have a hard time getting my breath. Now, given all that had happened, so much bad stuff, I knew it wasn't going to be anything like that. Nick could see I was anxious.

'Don't worry,' he kept saying. 'It'll be perfect.'

He did his best to arrange the church wedding I'd dreamed of and went and saw the priest at St John's but once he mentioned being divorced it was a non-starter. The priest asked to see both of us and suggested we have a blessing after the civil ceremony at the register office. We could still exchange solemn promises in church, in the eyes of God, he said.

The idea of getting married in the same register office as Nick and Lisa filled me with dread. It felt like a bad omen, as if we'd be jinxing things from the word go. I tried to explain but I'm not sure Nick really understood. Our wedding would be different, according to him, because this time he *wanted* to get married whereas first time round he'd practically had a gun to his head.

The day before the wedding I woke up sweating. I'd had a dream about arriving at the church in a big car with ribbons on the bonnet, bows fastened to the door handles. The car didn't feel right, though, and the ribbon was black. I was in a white dress with a long train, carrying a big bunch of cream lilies, like the ones you see at funerals. When the car stopped in front of the church there was nobody about. It was all locked up. I felt something tug at my dress and when I looked the train was caught in the car door. Only it wasn't a wedding car any more, it was a hearse, and it was on fire. Inside, banging on the windows, were my parents. Suddenly, they were a long way off. I started running towards them as fast as I could, tripping up in my heels, the train of the dress tangled round my ankles, but the car seemed to be getting further and further away. I was out of breath, sobbing, still clutching the lilies, ash all down the front of my dress. When I looked, the flowers were charred and black. I threw them on the ground. The hearse was a long way away now. I tried to shout for help but nothing came out.

I was in a panic, my heart thumping like mad. I couldn't get the images out of my head. It felt as if the dream was a warning, a sign that getting married was a mistake. I felt sick, full of dread.

I didn't say anything but Nick could see I was in a strange mood, quiet and preoccupied. I kept catching him giving me odd sideways looks, as if he was about to say something before changing his mind. Maybe he was too afraid to ask if everything was alright in case I said I couldn't go through with it and the wedding was off.

I had an appointment to get my hair done and he insisted on taking me. My hair was long, halfway down my back, still dyed jet black like my mum's. The hairdresser asked how I wanted it done. I'd seen a picture of Mum when she was young with her long hair worn loose with a soft curl in the end and that was what I asked for. The whole time I was in the hairdresser's Nick waited in the car. I don't think he dared let me out of his sight.

It was the same on our wedding day. The bad feeling from the day before wouldn't lift and Nick, picking up on it, I suspect, stuck like glue. Outside, it was a glorious sunny day but the atmosphere in the house was gloomy. While I was doing my make-up and getting ready Nick flitted about in the background, showering me with compliments.

'You're so beautiful,' he said. 'I can't believe you're going to be my wife.' I glanced at him reflected in the dressing table mirror. 'You look gorgeous,' he said. '*Mrs Benson.*'

That made me smile. 'We're not married yet.'

He looked at his watch. 'Two hours from now we will be.'

Gradually, the sense of unease that had hung about me since the day before started to lift. I tried not to think about my bad dream and what it did or didn't mean as I got into my wedding dress. I'd gone for something full-length, cream with a delicate lace trim on the bodice, and once I put it on I started to feel more like a bride. I had pink suede platform shoes and a little bag to match. I hadn't bothered with flowers, just an orchid pinned to the front of my dress. Michele was in a pink and white frilly frock, Nick in a plum-coloured velvet suit, his shirt open at the neck. He looked amazing and kept saying how beautiful I was, that he was the luckiest man alive. By the time we set off for the register office the last few misgivings I'd felt about marrying him had melted away. I reminded myself I was lucky to have someone like him. I'd found the man I wanted to be with for the rest of my life and he felt the same about me. As we drove through Walthamstow in the sunshine he reached across and took my hand.

'I've never seen you look lovelier,' he said.

His eyes seemed bluer than ever. The look on his face gave me butterflies. I knew how I felt about him; I was so, so in love. I told myself it would all work out and to stop worrying.

The civil ceremony was over in a flash and we headed to St John's where Fat June's Dad gave me away. I stood beside Nick in front of the priest making promises for the second time in the space of an hour, the huge church swallowing up our words. I meant it, about being faithful and staying with him for ever and, from the look on his face, I was certain he did too.

I'd been putting money aside for a honeymoon, saving my pennies, and had £30, which we reckoned would get us a couple of nights away. We decided on Cornwall with an overnight stop on the way down. We hadn't booked anywhere.

We got as far as Yeovil, in Somerset, and found a lovely guest house, big and imposing, with creeper on the front and roses at the door. We were in luck. They had just one room left.

A woman with coppery hair set in solid waves showed us upstairs. 'It's a big room, perfect for the three of you,' she said, throwing open the door to a bedroom done out in blue and white with views over the neat garden. Late evening sun streamed in through enormous sash windows. Nick's face fell.

'Oh, twin beds,' I said, trying not to laugh.

'I'm afraid it's all we have,' the woman said.

I don't suppose it crossed her mind that a couple with a toddler might be newlyweds. I glanced at Nick. He shrugged. We said we'd take it. After hours in the car, sweltering in the heat, I could probably have slept anywhere. The bed was cool with crisp cotton sheets. I must have been exhausted because almost as soon as my head hit the pillow I was in a deep sleep. Poor Nick wasn't so lucky. He'd only just got into bed when Michele started squawking and wouldn't settle. With her mother dead to the world, he had to take her in with him. It wasn't quite how he had pictured his wedding night.

In the morning, the same flame-haired woman from the night before served us breakfast, enormous fry-ups. We both marvelled at the eggs with their bright yellow yolks. They looked and tasted nothing like the ones we got at home.

Nick couldn't resist letting slip we were newlyweds.

'Oh, that's lovely,' she said. 'How long have you been married?'

'Let's see ... since yesterday.' He was grinning at me.

She looked mortified. 'And I gave you twin beds. On your wedding night!'

'Oh, it was fine,' I said, bright and breezy. 'Best night's sleep I've had in ages.'

Nick made a face. 'Out for the count she was, this one. Left me holding the baby. I had to wake her up this morning. Some honeymoon!'

The woman gave me a smile. 'There's not many men who'd take the little one so their wife can have an uninterrupted night. That's love, if you ask me. You've got a good one there, Mrs Benson.'

I thought so too.

We drove to Cornwall and found a hotel not far from Looe on the south coast. It was an old corn mill, higgledy-piggledy, all pale grey stone. Our room was quaint with beams and windows that weren't quite straight. The bathroom was lovely, done out in yellow. The whole place felt romantic, just right.

We even had a double bed!

I worked out how much money we had left, what we'd need for spending and petrol to get home, and reckoned we could afford to eat in the hotel that night. At the heart of the restaurant the old water wheel that once powered the mill, churned away. I felt as if I had stepped back in time.

'When people ask about the honeymoon let's just tell them about this place,' Nick said. 'I'll never live it down if word gets out we spent our wedding night in separate beds ...'

Next morning first thing, we drove to nearby Polperro. Whitewashed houses dotted the hillside and in the little harbour fishing boats bobbed side by side. The weather was perfect; clear skies, bright sunshine, sea more green than blue and a trawler chugging towards the horizon with seagulls chasing after it. We followed the coastal footpath out of the village where the view was breathtaking. It felt as if we were the only ones there. Nick hoisted Michele onto his shoulders and slung an arm round me.

'I want six children,' I said, ignoring what they'd said at the hospital about no more pregnancies after what I'd been through with Michele.

He looked amused. '*Six* children! That's a lot of nappies, Mrs Benson. Hundreds. Thousands, probably.'

If I was changing nappies for the next twenty years I wouldn't mind. It would be worth it.

Nick was laughing, bouncing Michele up and down as she giggled and hung onto his neck. 'Have you heard your mum?' he was saying. 'Six children. *Six children!*'

I was laughing too. In the sunshine everything felt easy, light. Just then I dared to believe that the way we were that day, so happy, not a care in the world, was how it was always going to be.

21.

I was married with a child I adored, a husband I loved. We were making a home for ourselves. On the face of things, life was good. Dig a little deeper, though, and it was a different story. Even in the early days of our marriage, I never really knew where I stood with Nick. He was up and down and all over the place – sometimes loving, full of plans for the future, sometimes acting as if he couldn't stand the sight of me. His mood could change at the drop of a hat. Dr Jekyll and Mr Hyde. Thinking about it now, the signs were there all along. My mum had been wise enough to see through him. Me, I was too naïve. I loved him and wanted to spend my life with him. I hadn't made my marriage vows for the fun of it and I certainly wasn't about to throw in the towel without doing everything I could to make things work. I really thought he felt the same. He said as much often enough and whenever he made promises, said how much he loved me, I believed him. For me, there was no one more convincing than Nick. He was good with words, very good, and back then, in my early twenties, I

125

hadn't really worked out that it's not so much what a person says as what they actually do that counts. He was my first proper relationship. I'd fallen for him when I was fifteen and was learning as I went along. I didn't know any better and, with my mum gone, there was no one I felt I could turn to and be sure they were on my side, no matter what. Things had changed with my sisters. We'd been close once and when my parents were alive we would all get together on a Saturday. Since the accident, everyone went their separate ways. It felt as if the family had fallen apart. Worse, I felt it was my doing. At times, I wished I could tell them I was struggling but I'd only been married five minutes and the thought of admitting my marriage was in trouble so soon filled me with shame. I didn't want my family to know what was really going on. And anyway, I don't suppose they'd have believed me since Nick was a different person, utterly charming, when other people were around. He could be stomping round the house in a rage but if someone knocked at the door he'd invite them in, happy as anything. Like I said, on the surface, at least, it must have looked as if things were pretty rosy.

I got it into my head that if Nick was unhappy it was down to me. It had to be. I was doing something wrong. When things were bad between us I went back over everything I'd said and done in the days beforehand, trying to work out how I had managed to sour things. I picked apart every little thing and, invariably, blamed myself.

I didn't look nice enough. I must have said something stupid, got on his nerves, somehow.

My opinion of myself was about as low as it could have

been. I could not shake the idea that I was the one at fault and if only I fixed whatever it was in me that was spoiling things between us everything would be fine. I told myself I had to do better, try harder. Be the perfect wife. Of course, at the root of all this were the feelings of guilt I had over the deaths of my parents.

In my heart, I knew I was being punished.

I couldn't help thinking it was what I deserved.

I never stopped thinking about my mum and dad, picturing them in their armchairs on opposite sides of the hearth, secret little smiles going back and forth, Dad bringing in a box of chocolates for Mum even when it wasn't a special occasion. Mum in and out of the kitchen, baking and cooking and making endless pots of tea. What they had was what I wanted with Nick. It was what I thought I could have, if only I stopped making such a mess of things.

Nick had started working for a bloke called Don Steele. It was still garage work, not that different from what he'd done before, but the hours seemed long and erratic. I never knew what time he was coming in. I'd enrolled to do State Registered Nurse training at Whipps Cross Hospital and what with that and looking after Michele, shopping and cooking and cleaning at home, there was a fair bit of juggling going on to make it all work. Not that I minded. I found I could manage as long as I took things one day at a time. My sister Jean helped out with looking after Michele, and I had friends willing to lend a hand too.

It didn't matter how busy a day I'd had I made a hot meal

for Nick coming in at night. He had always loved my cooking but, sometimes, when he was late and his tea had been in the oven a few hours, drying out, he'd take one look at it and tip the lot in the bin in disgust.

I didn't see why he couldn't just let me know if he was going to be held up at work.

'What's stopping you phoning to say what time you'll be in?' I'd say.

'So now I have to tell you every little thing, do I?'

'I don't want your tea ruined, that's all.'

'*You're* the one cooking. The oven's too hot, that's what's spoiling it.'

There was no point arguing, not when he seemed to have an answer for everything. And anyway, I couldn't help but think he probably had a point. I *was* the one cooking, not him.

22.

I was about to go to work one night and was rushing round the living room looking for my keys when Nick stopped me.

'Where do you think you're going?' he said.

I lifted up a magazine, let it drop, felt down the back of the chair. 'The hospital,' I said, rummaging in my bag.

He frowned. 'Looking like that?'

I didn't know what he was getting at. I had trousers on, a plain top. The three-quarter length trench coat I always wore for work.

'How come you're all done up?' he said, sounding suspicious.

I put my hand on the keys in the side pocket of my bag, buttoned up my coat and fastened the belt. 'I'm not *done up*. I'm wearing what I always wear.'

'You meeting someone?'

I looked at him, taken aback. 'Course not, don't be daft.' I was almost out the door when he got hold of me.

'Go and get changed,' he said. His voice had taken on a

hard edge.

'What?'

'You heard. Put your uniform on.'

I gazed at him. His face was like stone. 'I get changed at work, you know I do.'

'Yeah, I've been wondering about that.'

'What's that supposed to mean?'

'You go out of here looking like you're off to a club, you cow.'

I stared at him. 'A *club*?'

'If you're going to work – *if*, mind you – you won't mind getting your uniform on, will you?'

He was being ridiculous. 'I'm late as it is!'

'Better get a move on, then.'

I almost answered him back but the look on his face stopped me. Instead, I went and got changed.

At work, one of the other nurses had brought in a Victoria sponge cake. Homemade, oozing with jam and cream. It looked delicious. I watched as it was cut into thick slices, a slab placed in front of me. I knew I couldn't eat it. I'd been dieting for the past week, ever since Nick had told me I was getting fat.

'You're piling it on, Jenny,' he had said, giving me a look of disgust. 'God only knows what you're stuffing your face with but it's not attractive, not at all.'

As far as I knew I'd not got any heavier. My clothes felt fine, nothing straining. When I got on the scales I was just under eight stone, about the same as on our wedding day. I went through my wardrobe, dug out a pair of skin tight trousers I'd not worn for ages and tried them on. They still fit. Strange. I checked my reflection in the full-length mirror, trying to see what Nick saw when he looked at me. The more I scrutinised myself, the more convinced I became that I had got fat without realising it. I'd noticed my sisters gradually gaining weight over the years. Was I going the same way? I thought about my mum, always in heels because she was convinced flat shoes made her look dumpy. I had always been slim, bordering on skinny at times. Maybe the weight was creeping on without my noticing. I took off the trousers and put on a short fitted dress, studying myself from every possible angle. Common sense told me I hadn't changed, yet I couldn't get past what Nick had said. *Not attractive.* Looking in the mirror, I didn't like what I saw.

I started to watch what I ate.

I stared at the cake in front of me. All day, I had barely eaten. I was starving, my stomach crying out for something. As everyone else tucked in I felt my willpower crumble. I couldn't help thinking that the women I worked with were all a lot bigger than me yet didn't seem the least bit worried about their weight. No one else was counting calories or fretting about what a slice of cake was going to do to their figure, or what their husbands would say, so why should I?

The first bite was heaven. In no time, I'd eaten the lot, every last crumb. Straight away, the guilt set in. It was almost as if I could feel myself bulging with all that sugar and fat inside me. *Not attractive.* 'Oh God,' I thought, panic-stricken. 'When he sees me, he'll know.'

I went to the staff toilets, locked myself in a cubicle, bent over the bowl, stuck my fingers down my throat and threw up. Immediately, I felt better, back on track again. I'd had a moment of weakness but it was fine because in the space of a few seconds I had put things right. Nick would never know. It dawned on me I could eat what I liked and never get fat.

The next morning after Nick had gone to work I did a fry-up. Eggs, bacon, thick slices of buttered toast. I ate the lot and started on a packet of biscuits, only stopping when I couldn't manage another mouthful. Afterwards, I went to the bathroom and brought it all back up again. I felt powerful, in control. I really thought I'd found the answer. In fact, it seemed such an obvious solution I couldn't work out why it hadn't occurred to me before.

So desperate was I to please Nick, so convinced that getting his approval was the key to me feeling better about myself that I carried on, secretly gorging on food and making myself sick. It's a measure of how twisted my thinking had got by then that even though I knew what I was doing was dangerous, tantamount to self-harm, I kept going. From time to time, I made an effort to eat properly but all it took was a jibe about my looking fat or ugly or letting myself go and the madness would start up again. I didn't even come to my senses when I had so little food in my system I felt weak and ill and was fainting all over the place. I developed anaemia, yet still persisted in throwing up the bulk of what I ate. I was well and truly hooked. Inevitably, the euphoria I experienced initially proved short-lived and, before long, I felt worse about myself than ever. Sneaking off to vomit in secret became shameful. Disgusting. I thought I was the only person in the world to resort to such shocking behaviour. Little did I know that countless other people were battling the same self-destructive demon. It was only many years later, in 1992, when it came out that Princess Diana had a history of doing the same thing that I heard the term bulimia for the first time and discovered it was a recognised eating disorder.

All the time I was suffering from bulimia I remained convinced I was fat. I became obsessed with staying thin at any cost and wished I could stop eating altogether. I heard about a doctor who prescribed pills that suppressed your appetite, and went to see him. Despite what I thought there was no way I had a weight problem and even an unscrupulous doctor took some persuading to give me diet pills. I went back a few times, drinking as much water as I could beforehand, filling my pockets with coins, in an attempt to make myself appear heavier than I actually was when I got on the scales. It worked, and each time I came away with another prescription.

I was doing everything in my power to be the woman Nick wanted me to be and yet, no matter what I did, he still found fault. I didn't understand where I was going wrong. It never crossed my mind that he was the one with the problem, not me. To my mind, I was fat and ugly.

I hated myself.

I was in the kitchen when I heard the front door open. Nick, early for once. I'd done a bit of braising steak for his tea, nice thick gravy, the way my mum used to make it. The potatoes had just boiled and I drained them, mashed them with a fork, added lots of butter and salt, just how he liked them. Nick thudded into the kitchen and leaned against the wall as I buttered thick slices of bread. Straight away, I sensed he was in one of his moods. At least I could put a nice meal in front of him.

'What's that?' he said, as I lifted the meat out of the oven.

'Braising steak. One of your favourites.' It smelled really good.

'I thought you were doing sausage and mash.' There was an edge to his voice.

I glanced at him, caught the way he was staring at the food, the frown on his face, and felt a stab of panic. I'd bought steak instead of sausage, thinking it would be a treat. 'There's mash to go with it,' I said. It came out sounding like an apology.

I waited for him to say it didn't matter, steak would be lovely, but he kept quiet. As I spooned his food onto the plate it went through my head that I'd spoiled what could have been a perfectly good dinner. It was as if I couldn't get the simplest of things right. All I could think was that I didn't want a fight. More than anything, I wanted my husband to eat the meal I'd made for him, and enjoy it.

Nick went into the bathroom and I put his tea on the table in the living room. Michele was on the floor playing with wooden bricks, piling them up into a lopsided tower, toppling it over before she got very far. I crouched down and helped her make a stack that swayed and teetered. Delighted, she sent it flying, just as her father came into the room. I heard him make a tutting sound, irritated, as he stepped over the debris.

'Let's do another one,' I said, gathering up the bricks.

Nick was standing next to the table, as if in two minds

about sitting down.

I smiled up at him. 'Get your tea while it's hot,' I said.

He didn't move.

Brown sauce, I thought. He likes brown sauce. I scrambled to my feet. 'I forgot the sauce,' I said.

He picked up the plate and hurled it at me. It flew past, inches from Michele's head, and shattered against the wall, bits of food everywhere. I stared at him, too shocked to say anything. Michele started wailing. I bent and picked her up.

It seemed like an age before I was able to speak. 'What was that for?' I said.

'I'm sick of coming home to *this*!'

I hadn't a clue what he meant.

'Nick, I swear, I've no idea what I've done. What do you mean – sick of what?' I said.

'You! Everything!' He threw his hands in the air in fury. '*All of it*!'

Before I could say anything he turned and stomped off into the bedroom.

I settled Michele down and began picking up the bits of broken crockery, wiping down the paintwork. It wasn't that long since we had decorated and now there were streaks of gravy all down the wall. A single plate of food had managed to make an almighty mess. I still couldn't work out what had made him so angry.

A few minutes later he was on his way back along the hall, his footsteps sounding a good deal lighter. I picked up another sound. Whistling. His mood seemed to have changed completely. I held my breath and waited for him to come in and say sorry, put things right but instead, the front door went. I hurried out in time to see him stride off down the road and get into the car. He had changed out of his work things and put on one of his good suits. I recognised the shirt. It was the one I'd got him for his birthday, blue with a button-down collar. I stood at the window not knowing what to think as he drove away without a backward glance.

He had been home less than half an hour.

23.

There were two versions of Nick: Nice Nick and Nasty Nick. Nice Nick was funny and kind and sent long-stemmed red roses, gift-wrapped in a fancy box, and told me how much he loved me. Nasty Nick was cold and cruel with a vicious temper. I never knew which one was going to walk through the door so I tiptoed about on eggshells, desperate to keep the peace. Not that it made any difference. Nasty Nick was never far away and had a habit of popping up without warning. The weeks leading up to Christmas, when Michele was about four, were awful. There were so many rows about the stupidest things: he didn't like what I'd done with my hair; he wanted chips, not boiled potatoes; the cabbage was undercooked; the cabbage was overcooked. I took everything to heart and made frantic efforts to please him, not understanding that it didn't matter what I did, it wouldn't change a thing. He still stormed off, never a word about where he was going, and came home at all hours. A day or two later, once the dust had settled, Nice Nick would appear, full of apologies, carrying a big bunch of flowers. He would wolf down every bit of his meal, saying no one could cook as well as I did.

I was out of my mind, not knowing if I was coming or going. Despairing one day, the next full of hope that things would be alright after all.

It got so I knew the moment he came in whether or not he would be going straight back out again. I only had to look at him to see if he was in a temper, wanting to pick a fight. If he could engineer a row – and he always could – it gave him an excuse to clear off. Now, looking back, it's obvious what he was doing, although at the time I couldn't see it. He had me so tied up in knots I was convinced it was me being such a nightmare to live with that was driving him away.

Still, I wasn't altogether stupid. He wasn't getting done up, wearing his best stuff, a splash of aftershave, the cufflinks I'd got him as a wedding present, to go down the pub with his mates. It had to be another woman. Sometimes the phone went at home and when I picked it up whoever was on the other end hung up without saying anything. One time a woman had phoned asking for him but wouldn't leave her name. For a while I'd had my suspicions. When I confronted him, he denied it.

'Where did you get that idea?' he said, finding it funny. 'You know I love you.'

He put his arms round me and kissed the top of my head. 'Silly thing. Course there's no one else. It's you I want, always has been.'

Needless to say, this was Nice Nick doing the talking.

If I tackled Nasty Nick on the same subject he didn't take

it nearly as well.

'I'm going out so I have to be seeing someone else! You'd keep me under lock and key if you could! If you got your way I'd have no life!'

I was mad for accusing him, he said. A jealous cow. A raving lunatic. No wonder he had to get out of the house, with me accusing him of all sorts.

A couple of weeks before Christmas, he went out one night and didn't come back. Next morning I got ready, dropped Michele off at Jean's, and went to Whipps Cross Hospital where I was coming to the end of my SRN training. At lunchtime, I phoned the garage where Nick was working. Sure enough, he was there, busy with a client and not able to come to the phone, so the snooty-sounding receptionist said. It all seemed way grander than fitting tyres, which was what he actually did.

A couple of days went by and he came home to pick up some of his things. His boss, Don Steele, was letting him sleep on his settee until he got sorted out. As far as I was concerned, this Don Steele bloke was welcome to him.

'You're doing my head in, Jenny,' Nick said, sounding hard done by, as he shoved shirts into a bag and gave me a pleading look. 'I need some space.'

It seemed to me he already had all the space he needed, coming and going as he pleased. There had to be more to it than that for him to go and kip on a settee. 'If you're with someone else I'd rather you told me,' I said.

He shook his head, gave me a thunderous look. 'See, there you go again, accusing me. For Christ's sake, you drive me mental.'

'I'm not accusing you, I just want-'

He muttered something I didn't catch, flung the bag aside. 'WILL YOU STOP GOING ON AT ME!'

In a matter of seconds he had turned into Nasty Nick – hands clenched into fists, face twisted with rage. He towered over me, jabbed a finger in my face. 'See what you do? *See*?'

I kept quiet.

Grabbing his bag, he shoved me out the way and swept out of the room.

Once he'd gone, I sat on the edge of the bed trying to work out how I felt. I couldn't think straight. He was my husband and I wanted my marriage to work but the way Nick was – so chaotic, chopping and changing the whole time – it was impossible. He was gone now anyway. I didn't know what to do so I got on the phone to my sister, Lizzie.

'Nick's walked out,' I said, tearful all of a sudden.

Lizzie wanted to know what I'd gone and done now.

I honestly didn't know. 'He says he needs time on his own,' I said.

'Another woman, then, by the sound of things.'

I didn't say anything.

'You knew what he was like and you still married him,' Lizzie said, offhand. 'That's it, you've made your bed. You got to lie on it now. No one said married life's easy, you know. You get your ups and downs.'

Nick hadn't said anything about what I was supposed to do for money. I had enough to cover the rent for the next couple of weeks and that was about it. I thought about telling Lizzie I was down to my last few pounds but couldn't find a way of bringing it up and she never asked. She was busy saying she was up to her eyes, what with Christmas less than a fortnight away. Christmas. I'd done nothing about that yet.

'He'll be back,' she said. 'When it suits him. Whoever he's with, she won't put up with him for long. He's not going to change his ways, that one ...'

She was getting into her stride, going on about how I just had to get on with it. I wasn't really listening any more and when she paused for breath I cut in and said I'd better get off.

'I know it's hard, Jenny – that's life for you – but you got to get on with it. We all do. Don't think it's easy for me-'

I pretended someone was at the door and hung up.

I needed to think of a way of getting some money in. A friend at the garage where I used to work when I first met Nick said she'd let me know if there was the odd shift going. The week before Christmas I got a call one night to go in at six the next morning, a Saturday, and set off for work in the pouring rain in flip flops. I didn't have any boots and my nursing shoes were at the hospital. When I got to the garage, drenched, one of the other girls made some mean comment about me coming out dressed for summer. I made light of it, said I'd been rushing about so much I'd put the wrong shoes on, silly me. I didn't care. At the end of the day I'd earned enough to buy a pair of boots. Not for me, for Michele, for Christmas. Cute little red ones with white fur trim. I've still got them.

I didn't hear from Nick. I'd heard on the grapevine that the bloke he was staying with had a daughter. Young, pretty, long blonde hair. I managed to get a phone number and rang the house one night. The daughter answered. I got straight to the point.

'I hear you're sleeping with my husband,' I said.

She laughed. 'I don't know who's told you that.'

'Loads of people, as it happens. It's common knowledge.' That wasn't exactly true but it was what everyone was thinking.

'He works for my dad, that's all,' she said, not in the least bit rattled.

'I wasn't born yesterday,' I said.

'He's not stopping here for long. Just until he can get things sorted. Anyway, I thought you threw him out …'

'Is that what he said?'

I pictured him, Nice Nick, all innocent-looking, showing up with a few belongings in a bag, claiming his mad wife had chucked him on the street.

'It's none of my business anyway,' she said.

I was no further forward when I came off the phone.

By Christmas Day I was broke. Nick hadn't been near. There was very little food in the house: a few slices of bread, the last of the butter, a couple of eggs, tinned ham, and that was about it. Michele was poorly with some sort of bug and wasn't much in the mood for opening presents. Just as well, as she didn't have many. I gave her the cute red boots and she put them on with her pyjamas. Poor thing, all she wanted to do was sleep so I lit the gas fire downstairs, pulled the sofa forward and wrapped her in blankets so she was nice and warm. We stayed snuggled up together for most of the day. It didn't matter we had none of the usual Christmas paraphernalia. It was enough for me being with my little girl. I managed to get her to eat a boiled egg and soldiers at lunchtime while I filled up on endless pots of tea, saving what was left in the fridge for Boxing Day. In the afternoon some silly comedy was on the telly, one of those *Doctor* films with Leslie Philips and Simon Dee, and I lay there chuckling while Michele dozed in my arms. The fire lasted until teatime before I ran out of money for the meter and the place got cold. By about eight o'clock the house was freezing and I got into bed with Michele, the two of us huddling under the covers to keep warm.

24.

A few weeks after Nick walked out he breezed back in again. All that space he needed had started wearing thin. Not to mention sleeping on the settee. Or Don Steele's daughter with her long blonde hair. He missed me, he said. Missed Michele.

'Let's start again,' he said. 'Clean slate.'

I didn't know about that. I gave it some thought.

When I didn't answer, he said, 'You're my wife,' as if I needed reminding. 'I married you because I want to be with you. *For ever.*' I wouldn't look at him. He tugged at my hand. 'Come on, Jenny, I know you feel the same.'

I certainly used to. At one time. Whether it was how I felt now, I really couldn't say.

'We can't just give up,' he said. I looked at him. His eyes pleaded with me. That look of his was one I knew only too well. It managed to turn me inside out, stir up all kinds of stuff. In spite of everything I still had feelings for him. I really wished I could flick a switch and turn them off. All those weeks without him I had done everything in my power to draw a line under things. I just couldn't seem to do it.

In my heart, I loved him.

More than that, I felt I deserved him.

Lizzie's words came back to me, telling me I had to get on with it. *You've made your bed.* She was right about that. Something else she'd said was also niggling away. When I'd told her Nick had left she assumed it was down to me. *What have you done?* It brought all the old doubts back to the surface again. Now I had a chance to get things right, be the wife Nick wanted me to be. He stroked my hair, pushed it off my face.

'You're beautiful,' he said. 'You're all I want. We'll make it work, I promise.'

When he kissed me I didn't stop him.

I'd got my SRN qualification and registered with the Nursing Bank so I could do nights at whichever hospital needed staff. The night work suited me, mainly because Nick could look after Michele while I was out. We never seemed to have any money so I got a second job at a beauty salon, doing nails to start with. I started cleaning houses as well, fitting them in after my night shift. I would finish at the hospital first thing in the morning, go straight to one of my cleaning jobs, come home and get Michele ready for school, drop her off, and go to the salon. There wasn't a lot of time for sleep but I got by and the extra money came in handy.

When I got pregnant again I was overjoyed. Nick didn't say much when I broke the news. He didn't seem nearly as happy as he'd been when I was expecting Michele. All of a sudden he was back to his old ways, going out, coming in all hours, sometimes staying away a couple of nights at a time. I was tearing my hair out. Of course, I was sure it was my fault and agonised over what I'd done this time. Once or twice I caught him giving me filthy looks.

'You're a lot bigger this time,' he said, 'and you've got ages to go yet.'

He kept on making digs about my weight. Every bit of food I ate made me feel bad. I couldn't sit down to eat without the guilt making me want to stick my fingers down my throat and bring it all back up again. Not that I did, not with the baby to think about. I felt fat and unattractive. No wonder Nick was going out. I made a huge effort to look my best, always making sure my hair was done. I cooked his favourite meals, the roast dinners he was so fond of. It seemed the harder I tried the more he played up and picked fights and went out. While I sat on my own for hours on end waiting for him to come home I'd have imaginary conversations in my head, the two of us talking things over like sane, civilised adults.

'Nick, just tell me what's going on,' I'd say.

'I'm worried about how we're going to cope with the new baby,' he would say.

I would nod, relieved. He cared, that was all it was. 'We'll manage,' I'd say. 'We'll deal with today, never mind about tomorrow. It'll work out.'

He would hold me and we'd talk for hours, him promising to change his ways and be there for me and the baby.

These imaginary conversations were nothing like the ones we actually had.

Me: 'Don't go out.'

Nick: 'Not this again!'

Me: 'I don't even know what you're doing or who you're with.'

Nick: 'Meaning?'

Me: 'What's so important you can't stay in for once?'

Nick: 'Oh, for fuck's sake!'

Me: 'You're never here.'

Nick: 'Can you blame me, the way you go on the whole time!'

He was knocking me about. Slaps. Punches. Kicks. It didn't take much to set him off. Afterwards, once he'd calmed down, he would hold me and tell me how sorry he was. I hid the bruises and black eyes as best I could under make-up and came up with stories about walking into doors. When it came to what was really going on at home I kept quiet. It's hard to explain what being caught up in an abusive relationship does to you. Abusers are clever, manipulative. They know how to exploit vulnerability, twist things so everything becomes skewed and back to front. I wasn't good enough/nice enough/worthy enough. I was asking for it, getting what I deserved. Now, so many years on, I struggle to understand how I put up with such appalling cruelty. Thinking back, it doesn't seem real. The person I am today would be off at the first hint of bad behaviour. It took me a very long time to work out that the way I felt about myself because of the way my parents had died lay at the heart of it all.

To the rest of the world, Nick was the loveliest man. Funny, good company, always happy to run round here, there and everywhere for his friends. Nothing was too much trouble. No one else saw the side of him that flew across the room, got me by the hair and smashed my head against the wall. No one saw him hit me so hard I ended up on the floor.

I couldn't work out why I got Nasty Nick when everyone else got Nice Nick. The fact he was a different man when it came to the rest of the world only served to make me even more certain it was something in *me* that tipped him over the edge.

When I say no one knew what was going on, that's not quite true. I did try talking to Lizzie. She didn't want to know.

'What you doing having another baby with him if he's as bad as you say?' she said. 'You want your head examined.'

At the doctor's for one of my regular antenatal check-ups my GP weighed me, checked my blood pressure and did an examination. Having had pre-eclampsia when I was expecting Michele, I was being closely monitored. So far, four months into my pregnancy, there was nothing to worry about. Not where the baby was concerned, anyway. The doctor was more interested in the bruising on my face – which I hadn't covered up with make-up half as well as I thought I had – and finding out why my back was black and blue.

When he asked how I'd ended up in such a state I gave a shrug. The night before last I'd been in the kitchen when Nick came in from work, spoiling for a fight. What set things off I've no idea – probably me having the gall to ask if he was staying in for a change. One minute I had my back to him, draining the potatoes, steam billowing up. Next thing the pan went clattering out of my hands, scalding water splashing my arms. I yelped and scrabbled for the tea towel on the bench. Before I reached it he had me by the hair and was yanking me backwards, lifting me off my feet. I felt something give, a clump of hair come out, and threw a punch to get him off me but he kept on pulling hard until my head was bent so far back I thought my neck would snap. I looked up at him, tears running down my cheeks, into my hair. He put his face close to mine and spat something out about being sick of coming home to me going on at him. I was gasping, my chest heaving. 'On and on and on,' he was saying. 'Mad cow, you're doing my head in.' He was swearing, calling me names, for what seemed like ages before he let go, although it was probably only a few seconds. When you've got adrenaline pumping through your body it's hard to keep track of time. Eventually, I felt his grip loosen and he shoved me away, so hard I landed face down on the floor and smacked my head on the tiles. Blood ran from a gash on my brow while I lay still on the cold floor, not daring to move until I heard him go out again. Once the front door shut I went into the bathroom and washed my face, put a dressing on the cut on my head. I ran a bath and lay in it until the water went cold. Then I cleaned up in the kitchen. A few hours later he came back in and got into bed, held me so tight I thought he would squeeze the breath out of me.

'I'm so sorry,' he said, over and over. 'I don't know why I do it. I love you. I love you so much.'

I was wide awake, tears streaming down my face, but I kept my eyes screwed shut. I wished we could have one of those imaginary conversations, the ones where we got things sorted out, no shouting, no getting thumped, but I was too scared to open my mouth in case I said the wrong thing.

In the surgery, the doctor was waiting for me to speak. He had a kind face, lined, dark hair with a bit of a curl at the ends, like my dad. It was no good, I couldn't tell him.

'It's just, you know …' I said, eventually, not looking him in the eye.

For a moment he said nothing. On the wall behind him was a chart showing the body's internal organs. When I was doing my SRN training we had one just like it in the classroom.

'Alright,' he said, writing something on my notes. 'All I'll say is you don't have to put up with it. If you ever need me to speak up for you, I'd be happy to.' He looked up and caught my eye. I hadn't said a word, yet I could tell he knew exactly what was going on at home. 'If you decide to go to court I'll be a witness…' He let the thought hang in the air. 'Come back and see me and we can talk about how I can help you.'

For one brief, crazy moment I thought about blurting it all out. *Go on*, a voice in my head said. *What's stopping you?* What *was* stopping me? Probably a deep-seated belief that what was going on at home was my own fault. I shook my head. If I told him he would find out what I was really like – the vile, ugly person Nick told me I was.

It was better to keep quiet.

25.

The bedroom light snapped on. Seconds later the covers were flung back and I was dragged out of bed. Nick, smelling of beer and cigarettes, stood over me in his good blue suit. I blinked up at him, the light hurting my eyes. Gone four, according to the alarm clock on the bedside table. His shirt was buttoned up wrong and I wondered where he'd been half the night. I had a sudden urge to tell him to clear off back to his girlfriend or wherever it was he'd been but I didn't dare provoke him, not when I could see he was already worked up. I was five months gone and had the baby to think about. I made a move to get up and without warning he lashed out, kicking me hard in the stomach. I gasped and scuttled across the floor on my hands and knees. He came after me, grabbing my nightdress, ripping the sleeve. My heart was thumping as I curled into a ball, hands over my stomach, praying he'd leave me alone. Instead, he got me by the shoulders, spun me onto my back and started laying into me, aiming kicks at my stomach. He was in a rage, acting like a madman. I thought he would never stop.

I lost the baby.

A little girl.

At the hospital, when they told me, I felt numb. They took me into theatre and did a D & C procedure to remove any tissue left behind in the uterus. As soon as I came round I asked about going home.

I could barely stand up so I got them to phone a cab. A porter took me down to the entrance in a wheelchair and waited for it to come. I had a coat on over my nightie, bare legs, flip flops. The driver helped me into the passenger seat at the front and didn't say a word all the way. It must have been obvious I wasn't in the mood to chat. When I got home Nick paid the cab, put the kettle on and made some tea. I took mine and went to bed. He could see I was in a bad way, hanging onto the walls to stay upright. He didn't ask about the baby, didn't need to.

He could see by looking at me there wasn't a baby.

Not any more.

A few days later my brother, Alf, showed up at the house. It was a surprise to open the door and see him. Alf wasn't one for calling round. Somehow he'd got wind that Nick was beating me up. I reckon Lizzie must have put two and two together when I lost the baby and told the rest of them she didn't think it was an accident. I was still in a bad way, finding it difficult to walk. Alf followed me down the hall as I shuffled along, using the wall as a support. In the living room he looked me up and down.

'What the bloody hell's he been doing to you?' he said. I

shook my head. 'Right. What's his number?'

He phoned Nick at work and told him to get back home. While we waited I put him in the picture about him some of what had been going on.

He listened, grim-faced. 'Why the hell didn't you say something?'

I didn't know how to, that was why. I thought about Mum and Dad getting killed and how ever since I felt I was being punished. Putting it into words in a way that made sense to anyone else was beyond me. I ended up spouting the same stuff Lizzie had said about making my bed and having to lie on it. Alf looked at me as if I was mad.

'Who told you that? What a load of bollocks!'

When Nick came home he acted all innocent, trying to make light of things. 'Am I in bother? What have I done now?'

Alf wasn't in the mood. 'Are you blind?' he said, pointing at me. 'Look at the state of her.' Nick glanced at me and looked away again sharpish. 'This can't go on,' Alf said. 'You ever lay a hand on her again and I'll come down on you like a ton of bricks. You hear me?'

Nick nodded, muttered something about being under a bit of pressure at work.

Alf tore into him. 'You'll know what pressure feels like if you touch her again!' He looked at me. 'If you want a divorce, I'll pay.'

My jaw must have hit the floor. Lovely as my brother was, he was notoriously tight when it came to money. I always said he was so mean he wouldn't give you the steam off his tea and I wasn't joking. If Alf was willing to stump up the cash for a divorce things were about as serious as they could get. Nick was taken aback too, never for a minute thinking he might get his marching orders from my brother, of all people.

Alf's visit did the trick. Nick sat me down, full of apologies. 'I don't want to lose you,' he said. 'I don't know what gets into me.'

Just like that, the beatings stopped. He was back on his best behaviour. There was no mention of the baby I'd lost. No one said a word about her. It was as if she had never existed. I mourned her in silence, keeping my feelings to myself.

26.

Children meant the world to me. I still wanted more but couldn't seem to get pregnant again. Tests showed I had cysts on my ovaries. The plan was to deal with them and put me on a fertility drug to boost my chances of conceiving. I was back and forwards to the hospital but before they did anything I had to have a pregnancy test, a formality, since it was obvious to everyone I wasn't pregnant. In those days, you had to wait a week for the results to come through. I already knew what they were going to say. It was simply a case of having the negative test confirmed before the treatment could get underway. Even then, I'd been warned it could take a while for me to get pregnant.

My friend, Pearl, was round for lunch the day I phoned the hospital for my results. She heard me say, 'Oh so it's positive, then.'

Pearl sat, open-mouthed, fork in mid-air.

Even though it was the last thing I expected to hear I felt completely calm. It was what I wanted, after all. 'OK, thanks for letting me know.' I put the phone down. 'Turns out I'm pregnant, after all,' I said.

Pearl stared. 'How did you manage that?'

I burst out laughing. 'Usual way, I suppose.'

'But … you had no idea?'

I really hadn't. Not a hint of nausea – nothing to give the game away. The baby I was carrying had managed to sneak up on me.

'I can't believe you're so calm,' Pearl said. 'Not now it's all going to happen a lot faster than you thought.'

The sooner the better, as far as I was concerned. More than anything, I wanted a baby. I beamed at Pearl, still looking bewildered, her fork up a height.

'Are you planning to eat with that or just wave it about?' I said.

Finding out I was expecting again was just what I needed for me to finally get to grips with my destructive eating habits. The little person growing inside me represented love and happiness and I wasn't about to risk doing any damage. From then on I made sure I ate properly.

I knew from the outset I was having a boy. When I was pregnant with Michele everything I bought was pink. This time all the baby stuff was blue, even the cute little coming home outfit for when he was born. Nick was over the moon and watched amused as the blue baby clothes piled up.

'I hope you're right about this,' he said, 'or we're going to be sitting with a load of stuff we don't need.'

As soon as I knew I was pregnant I arranged an epidural for the birth. After what I'd been through having Michele, I couldn't take any chances. I was promised, no matter what, I'd get my epidural. On the evening of September 4 I started having contractions. Nick could see I was in pain and wanted to take me to the hospital but I wasn't ready to go. Next morning I had a bath, washed my hair and did my make-up, thinking having a baby was no reason not to make an effort. By the time I finished I felt like a film star. Nick took me to hospital where I'd hardly got settled in bed when a big, burly nurse appeared and took it into her head I'd feel better for a nice cooling wash. Before I knew what was happening a soggy great sponge was slapped in my face. So much for my make-up!

As the pain kicked in, I asked about the epidural and was told there was a bit of a problem. They'd done so many that day already the anaesthetist was no longer available. I couldn't believe it.

'I can't have this baby without an epidural!' I said, panicking.

The nurse, the same one who'd whacked me with a wet sponge, tried to reassure me. 'We'll look after you, don't worry.'

'I was promised an epidural!'

She patted my hand. 'Try to stay calm,' she said. 'Nice deep breaths.'

Deep breaths! Fat lot of use they were going to be. My contractions had got worse and the pain was unbearable. They gave me gas and air, so-called laughing gas, to take the edge off things but it wasn't helping at all. When I complained I was told to stick with it. I was in a bad way, tears running down my cheeks. I didn't know which way to turn. I pressed the mask over my face and kept an eye on the clock on the wall facing me. Thirty seconds went by. Nothing. Pain shot through me. A minute passed. I bit on the mouthpiece in distress. If this was supposed to be laughing gas I definitely wasn't seeing the funny side.

'It's not doing a thing!' I said, desperate.

'Try again,' Nick said, gripping my hand hard.

Just then I noticed the red indicator light on the machine blinking. It was empty! No wonder I wasn't getting any relief.

'It's no good, it's not working,' I said, gasping, chucking the mask on the bed in frustration.

Nick had seen enough. When a doctor appeared he got hold of him and told him I needed proper pain relief. I was given a massive dose of Pethidine, enough to knock me half senseless. Hours went by. In the corridor outside the delivery room Nick paced up and down.

'I'll get your husband,' one of the nurses said, hurrying away, when the baby finally decided to come.

'Noooooooooooooo! I don't want him!'

'You don't want him here for the birth?'

'I never even wanted him there for the conception!' Whether that was me or the Pethidine talking I'm not sure. A bit of both, probably.

She went and got him anyway.

Just before midnight on September 5, after I'd been in labour for more than twenty-four hours, the baby's head appeared. Something wasn't right. The cord was wrapped around his neck, twice, strangling him. It was pandemonium as they struggled to shove him back inside so they could get the cord off him. At six minutes past midnight, on September 6 he was finally born. We had already chosen a name: Michael. I watched them whisk him away. The Pethidine they'd given me had knocked me out but there was no mistaking the fact my baby was blue, like a Smurf, and from the way everyone was carrying on it was obvious something was seriously wrong. He wasn't making a sound. Not breathing. He seemed utterly lifeless. Nick looked at me, ashen, squeezing my hand so hard I thought he'd crush me as the doctor began suction to clear the baby's lungs. I lay still, not daring to take my eyes off him, in tears, sweat dripping off me. The room had gone eerily quiet, no one saying anything. It seemed an awful long time before the doctor nodded. Michael had started breathing. The relief we felt was short-lived. As the suction tube was removed half of it got left behind, lodged in his tiny lung. You could have cut the atmosphere with a knife as the medical team went into a huddle, trying to work out what to do next. Now, despite the Pethidine, I was fully alert.

'The baby needs specialist care. We're going to take him to the Queen Elizabeth,' the doctor announced.

The Queen Elizabeth was a good hospital, as far as I knew, but it was in Hackney. Miles away. 'You're not taking him anywhere,' I said.

'We don't have anyone available here to do the surgery,' the doctor said.

Alarm bells rang. I knew from the amount of Pethidine I'd been given that Michael must be awash with the stuff. If they put him under he wouldn't survive. 'He's not having surgery –

are you trying to kill him?' I was hysterical.

'We don't have the expertise here-' the doctor started to say.

'Then get someone *in* – and *fast*! If anything happens to that baby I will hold you personally responsible.'

There were panic stations, people running in and out. It turned out they did have a specialist able to handle the procedure, after all, but he was off-duty. They were doing all they could to track him down.

All we could do was wait and hope. Time ticked by. Nick went out for some air. He was pacing about when a big swanky Daimler screeched up to the entrance and the passenger door flew open. A silver-haired man jumped out and went running into the hospital before the car had even come to a complete standstill. Apparently, this was the specialist called in to remove the tube embedded in Michael's lung.

Nick came back in and we sat in silence waiting for news. Eventually the specialist came to tell us everything had gone well.

'You're very lucky,' he said. 'We managed to remove the tube using suction. No need for surgery.'

'No,' I said. '*You're* the lucky ones. He wasn't born with a tube in his lung. There was nothing wrong with him until I came into this hospital.'

Nick was badly shaken up. He looked worse than me; red-eyed, white-faced, dazed.

'That's it, you're never going through that again,' he kept saying, over and over.

Michael weighed in at 7lbs 8oz, a real little bruiser. Where

Michele was pretty and placid, Michael screamed and waved his fists about. He had the most amazing eyes, though – like deep blue limpid pools. As I held him for the first time the love I felt for him washed over me, extraordinary and intense, just as it had when Michele was born.

Back on the ward I was desperate to get some rest but in the bed next to mine was a Peruvian woman, very sweet, broken English, clearly having a hard time breastfeeding. Whenever she tried to feed her baby she shrieked in pain. 'Eee! Eee! Eee! Eee! Eee! Eee! Eee! Eee! Eee!'

It wasn't exactly relaxing.

Two days after Michael was born I started haemorrhaging. Some of the afterbirth had been left behind and there was a risk it would go bad and poison my whole system. No one had thought to mention this to me. All of a sudden it was all systems go. They needed to get it out – and quickly. I was rushed to theatre for an emergency D & C, the same nurse who'd given me an empty gas and air cylinder when I was in labour running alongside the trolley trying to convince me everything was under control. I wasn't inclined to believe her.

When I came round, I couldn't help thinking it was doing me more harm than good being in hospital. What they'd do to me next was anyone's guess. I lay in bed, groggy, feeling sore.

'Eee! Eee! Eee! Eee! Eee! Eee! Eee! Eee! Eee!' The Peruvian woman in the next bed was off again.

That did it.

I got dressed, discharged myself, and took Michael home. Only later did I discover that nothing about the circumstances of his birth, or my emergency D & C, had gone on my notes.

27.

Michael was still a baby when Nick got it into his head he wanted us to buy a place of our own. There was a terraced house in Newbury Park that needed work, he said. It was perfect. I wasn't keen. I liked it where we were. We'd got the house in Forest Road looking nice and the rent was low – plus it held a lot of memories for me.

'That's exactly why we should move,' Nick said. 'All those memories, they're about the past. We should be thinking about the future. *Our* future.'

I was thinking about my mum and dad and how, silly as it may sound, being in their old house was my way of staying close to them. Nick had a pretty good idea what was going on inside my head.

'They're not here,' he said. 'It's just a house, bricks and mortar. They'd want you to get on with your life.'

He had a point. They weren't there. Same as they weren't in the cemetery. When I thought about it, the memories tied up in the house involved huge amounts of loss and heartache.

Maybe hanging onto it wasn't good for anyone and the best thing all round was to let go and make a fresh start.

I worked like crazy, doing as many hospital shifts as I could, to get the deposit together. The house was on the market for £26,000, which seemed like a huge amount of money. The idea of a mortgage when we'd been used to paying £13 rent a week and having the security of a council house scared me and even after we had an offer accepted I lost my nerve. We must have pulled out of the sale three or four times but it seemed the vendor really wanted us to have it because each time I got cold feet he dropped the price and Nick managed to talk me round again.

In the end, after months of it being on and off and on again, the sale went through.

We took our time doing the place up before moving in. Most days I went round there with Michael in the pram and got on with whatever needed doing. Michael was the most angelic-looking baby but, at eighteen months old, he had a wicked streak. I never knew what he was going to do or say next. Strangers constantly came up to admire his blond curls and big blue eyes. Always, my heart was in my mouth, hoping he wouldn't misbehave.

One lovely sunny day we were on our way to the new house, Michael in the pram, a dummy in his mouth, when I spotted two nuns coming our way. I prayed they wouldn't stop. Of course, they did. Michael gazed up at them.

'What a beautiful child,' one of the nuns said, putting her face close to his.

Michael reached up and took his dummy out. 'Piss off!' he

said, beaming.

The smile slid off the poor nun's face.

'I'm so sorry,' I said, mortified. 'I've no idea where he got that from.'

I quickly pushed his dummy back in and hurried off before he had a chance to show off any other expletives he'd managed to pick up.

Nick and I had our work cut out to get the house looking the way we wanted it. The previous owner, an elderly man, had bought it new in the nineteen-thirties and not done much in the intervening years, other than decorate. When we stripped layers of wallpaper off the front room we found all the builders' workings-out scrawled over the walls.

There were three bedrooms and big bay windows top and bottom at the front. The kitchen was tiny and basic with a sink and a few units. Nick gutted it. The bathroom and separate toilet were cramped little spaces so he knocked through to make one good-sized room. My sister Christine was getting a new bathroom and we bought her old suite. It was yellow, just like the one in the hotel on our honeymoon, which pleased me no end. It was the first house I'd lived in with an upstairs bathroom.

'This is just the start,' Nick would say. 'One day we'll have a big detached place, set back, driveway at the front.'

I had always wanted a pink house. When I told him, he said, 'You can have whatever colour you want. Swimming pool round the back, flash car on the drive.'

It felt good, making plans, even if they did seem pie in the sky. I began to believe we could achieve anything we wanted if we set our minds to it.

I still don't know why things went so wrong, so fast.

We finally moved in and were in the throes of unpacking and getting things straight when Nick came downstairs in the plum velvet suit he'd worn for our wedding and announced he was off out. The front door banged shut behind him. On the stairs was a note saying I thought more about Michael than I did about him. Where he'd got that from I had no idea. It was an excuse and a poor one at that. Without warning, he was back to his old ways, out every night, coming in all hours, knocking me about.

He was working for his brother-in-law, selling cars. Sometimes, he'd leave photos lying around taken in some club or other, a woman draped all over him. When I asked what was going on, he shrugged and said it was part of the job. He was *entertaining clients*. The women in the pictures worked at the various clubs he went to and getting snapped with them didn't mean anything. How he managed to keep a straight face talking such rubbish was beyond me. It didn't matter what I said he stuck to his guns. It was *work*, he said – not that he expected me to understand.

I understood perfectly well.

He didn't like it when I stood up to him and showed it with his fists. Plenty of times I went to work with a black eye or my face all swollen. At the time, I was working at a hospital with a lovely matron I called Aunty Eileen and when I came in black and blue she would take me to one side and make me tea. She never asked what was going on. I don't suppose she had to.

I was certain Nick was seeing other women, not even being careful about it. Word got back that he'd been seen with some woman in his car. When I confronted him he denied it.

'Oh, that was Heidi,' he said. 'Just some silly young girl I was giving a lift home to, that's all.'

He was so keen to make out he had nothing to hide he told me too much about her. She was German and lived on such-and-such street in Bethnal Green. The next day, I got on to my cousin, Linda. 'I need to find this woman he says he's not seeing, find out what's really going on.'

Linda said she'd come with me

Heidi had to live in just about the longest street in Bethnal Green. We trudged from one end to the other, knocking on doors, asking for her. Linda was dubious.

'What if we find her?' she said.

'That's the whole point!'

'I don't want no trouble.'

'I'll talk to her, that's all.'

We'd been all the way along one side and worked our way back up the other until we were almost back where we'd started. I was losing hope when a woman said she knew Heidi and gave us the house number. It was one we'd already been to. We went back.

This time, a young girl, eighteen or so, came to the door. Dark hair, boyish-looking. Moustache sprouting on her top lip.

'It's Heidi I'm looking for,' I said, not thinking for a moment this was the right girl.

'I'm Heidi,' she said.

I looked at Linda. She raised an eyebrow.

'Do you know who I am?' I said. She shook her head. 'You should do. You're sleeping with my husband.'

She looked startled. 'He said you're getting divorced. He showed me the papers.'

'I haven't even started divorce proceedings yet but I'll see you in court when I do,' I said.

'I don't know why you're cross with me,' she said, getting shirty all of a sudden. 'I'm not the only one he's been out with.'

'I'm cross with *you* cos you're the silly cow I've caught him with,' I said. 'I'm cross with *you* because while he's spending on *you* I can't afford to spend on his two children. And I'm cross with *you* because you knew he was married.'

'We don't do anything,' she spluttered. 'Just talk and … drink coffee.'

Nick had never drunk a cup of coffee in his life.

I was livid. 'Can't you find someone your own age? Is it because you've got a moustache like a fella?'

She flushed. 'There's no need to be so insulting.'

'You keep going out with other people's husbands, expect to be insulted,' I said.

I told Nick I wanted a divorce. He denied everything. Heidi was a kid, he said. Not even good-looking. I'd got the wrong end of the stick.

I still wanted a divorce.

We hadn't been out for ages but in an effort to smooth things over he took me for a drink. He shouldn't have bothered. When we walked into the pub every woman in the place swivelled round and stared at the pair of us. We had one drink and went somewhere else, where he left me with a couple of mates of his while he went to the bar.

'So, which one are you, then?' one of them asked.

I held his gaze. 'Me? I'm the one he's married to,' I said.

His face was a picture.

28.

If I wanted a divorce I was going to have to get evidence. I hired a private detective and had Nick followed, and before long knew exactly what he was doing – and who he was seeing. Once I had the proof I needed I began divorce proceedings. Nick alternated between writing letters begging for another chance, and, when I wouldn't budge, beating me senseless. For months he dodged every effort to serve him with the divorce papers. It was horrible and stressful and I got really skinny again, like I had when my parents were killed. My stomach was in knots the whole time and I was getting terrible pains. It turned out the lack of food in my system had caused an acid build-up resulting in gallstones. I was going to have to have my gall bladder removed. Nick said he would look after the children while I was in hospital.

The night before the operation, he came home in a temper and picked a fight.

'I'm not looking after your kids,' he said. *Your kids*. 'Get one of your boyfriends to do it.'

There were no boyfriends. 'You can't just drop me in it!'

'I can do what I like. It's not me that wants a divorce.'

He hit me so hard I almost passed out. Stars danced in front of my eyes. Blood poured down my cheek. A flap of skin hung loose under my eye. My face throbbed. Nick stood over me ranting and raving, calling me all sorts. I started counting inside my head, trying to block out the pain. One, two, three. I got to 500 before he went, slamming the door so hard it's a wonder it stayed on its hinges. I rang my sister, Jean, asked if she would have the kids while I went to the hospital where they did their best to stick my face back together.

A few hours later I was back in the same X-Ray department before being taken down to theatre for my gall bladder op. The last thing I remember before I went under was the anaesthetist giving me a telling off for having false eyelashes on. I started to say they weren't false but didn't get as far as the end of the sentence. Anaesthetic doesn't half work fast. Once you're under you're totally out of it until they bring you round again. In theory, anyway. In my case, I was paralysed, not able to move a muscle, but at the same time fully aware of what was going on. I felt the heat of the theatre lamps, heard the surgeon run through the procedure and say he didn't think the usual L-shaped incision was suitable in my case.

'She's such a tiny thing and she's only young,' he said. 'I don't want to ruin her body. I'm going to cut around the waist instead.'

I lay there, panicking, no way of letting him know I wasn't quite as under as everyone seemed to think. As the surgeon made the cut a searing pain went through me. I must have passed out because it was the last thing I remembered before they brought me round and I started babbling about being awake during the op. The nurses must have thought I was delirious until I relayed exactly what I'd heard. I don't suppose that went on my notes either.

I'd made it clear when I was admitted I didn't want Nick visiting me but he turned up anyway and charmed his way in.

'What happened to your face?' he said, pulling up a chair next to the bed.

I ignored him.

He told me he had emptied the bank account. 'I don't know what you're going to do about paying the mortgage,' he said. 'There's nothing left. I've spent it all.'

I was so upset the asthma I'd developed after my parents died flared up and I couldn't get my breath. I was heaving and gasping. The nurses came running and clamped an oxygen mask on my face. Nick patted my hand. 'Poor thing, she gets so upset when it's time for me to go,' he said.

The worst thing about being in hospital was not seeing the children. I was desperate to speak to them. The ward Sister said I could phone Jean as long as I kept the call short. She walked me to the pay phone. 'No getting worked up,' she said. 'I don't want another asthma attack.'

Jean let rip. 'No you can*not* speak to them,' she said. 'And don't ever expect me to look after them again because this is the last time! I'm not doing another thing for you, you little cow. Sort out your own mess in future.'

'Why, what's happened?' I said.

'We've had Nick round here, that's what.'

He had shown her his back, covered in scratches, claiming I'd gone for him. Swore blind he hadn't laid a finger on me. I'd whacked myself with a phone book, he said, just to get him in trouble. I was off my head, crazy, a nutcase – so hell bent on getting a divorce I'd do anything. My sister had swallowed it all. I could feel myself getting worked up again, struggling to breathe.

'I never touched him!' I said, my voice rising.

'You're as bad as each other!'

I slumped against the wall. The Sister, watching from a few feet away, hurried over and took the receiver off me.

'Are you trying to kill your little sister?' she told Jean. 'Because you're going about it the right way. I don't want to hear another word from you.'

I couldn't stop thinking about what Jean had said. Maybe I *was* crazy. The next day when the doctor did his rounds I showed him my face and asked if there was any chance I had split it open myself without realising it. He gave me an odd look and said it wasn't remotely possible.

It was only when I got home that Michele restored my sanity. My ten-year-old daughter, hearing her father's raised voice, had crept downstairs and seen him attack me and, as I lay face down on the floor, pull up his shirt and rake his nails down his own back.

It wasn't me that was crazy.

29.

A date was set for the divorce hearing. Nick didn't turn up. My solicitor pressed on anyway, outlining the infidelity and violent behaviour, backed up with evidence from the private detective, my doctor and numerous hospital reports. The judge had no hesitation granting a decree nisi on the grounds of cruelty and adultery. He also made an order to oust Nick from the house. It wasn't easy getting him out. He hung about until the last minute when the locks were about to be changed and finally went, grumbling all the way about how unfair it all was. Once he was gone I breathed a sigh of relief – but not for long. Three weeks later, Nick took me back to court, determined to get the order overturned. I felt confident the law was on my side.

Nick shuffled into court, coughing, wearing his oldest, scruffiest clothes. His hair was dirty and he looked in need of a good wash. I couldn't work out why he'd come as a rough sleeper when I knew full-well his sister Paula was putting him up. I soon found out. According to him, he was having to sleep in someone's garage because he had nowhere else to go. I couldn't believe my ears.

He'd got himself a lawyer, a woman with a loud grating voice and startling blue eyeshadow, who made out he was the injured party. He was a good father, she said, committed to providing a home for his family. His main concern was to remain under the same roof as his children. Meanwhile, my actions had left him homeless and were having a detrimental effect on his health. All the time she was on her feet, Nick nodded and coughed and patted his chest.

I was dying to have my say and set the record straight.

'There's a very good reason an order was made to oust him from the family home,' I said, once she started questioning me. 'He kept putting me in hospital.'

'Come now, Mrs Benson,' she said, 'all this talk of violence is pure fabrication on your part, isn't it?'

I pointed to the livid scar under my eye. 'Does this look like fabrication to you?'

She rifled through her papers. 'Aren't you inventing stories because you're *jealous* of your husband going out with other women?' She gave me a pitying look. '*That's* the truth, isn't it?'

'The *truth* is he's been knocking me about for years!' I was starting to run out of patience.

Nick, a picture of innocence, gazed straight ahead.

His lawyer raised an eyebrow. 'I think we all know that is far from being the case.'

I waited for my solicitor to say something but all the fight seemed to have gone out of him. It was obvious which way things were going and I wasn't at all surprised when the judge sided with Nick.

'I can't see that Mrs Benson is in any danger if we allow her husband to move back into the matrimonial home,' he said.

I jumped up. 'Are you mad?!'

He glared at me. 'I must ask you to sit back down.'

'You let him move back in and you'll have to find somewhere else for me and the children,' I shouted, 'because I am *not* staying under the same roof as him!'

'I can see feelings are running high but I see no reason why your husband should not move back into the family home. It may well be in the best interests of the children-'

Nick, scenting victory, grinned at his lawyer. I lost it. 'Are you deaf? I will NOT live with that man! If he moves in I'm taking the kids and leaving – so you'd better work out where you're putting us.'

The judge had gone scarlet. 'This is your final warning, Mrs Benson.'

'I couldn't care less!' I threw my arms up in the air. 'I AM NOT SHARING A HOUSE WITH HIM!'

He had me taken to a holding cell, shouting and screaming. I didn't shut up until someone came to tell me the order ousting Nick from the house remained in place.

The children were sleeping. It was late, gone eleven, but I was wide awake. I had already locked up but went round checking the doors again before going upstairs. All the windows were shut and the place felt stuffy and airless. Sweat ran down my back. I sat at the top of the stairs, alert, a carving knife in my hand. Nick had been on the phone shouting the odds yet again about me having him chucked out of the house.

'It's as much my house as yours,' he said.

Not for much longer. It was in the process of being re-mortgaged and put in my name, something he had agreed to.

'You're stopping me seeing my kids,' he said.

I wasn't. He could see the kids whenever he wanted. 'Any time you want to see them just let me know,' I said.

'Who do you think you are telling me when I can and can't see them? I'm their father!'

I wanted to say it was about time he started acting like one. The last time he was meant to come round to see the kids they'd been at the front window watching out for him for ages and he hadn't shown.

'I'm not telling you anything, I'm just-'

'I'll be round later, then,' he said.

'Not tonight.'

'Why, got your boyfriend round, have you?'

There was no boyfriend. 'Just give me a bit of notice,' I said.

'You want *notice*?' he snapped. 'Here you go then – I'll be round later to burn the fucking place down! With you in it.' He paused. '*And* them.'

The line went dead. My hands were shaking. I got straight on to the police and reported him.

'He's threatening to kill us,' I said, 'and I don't doubt he means it.'

The officer I spoke to was sympathetic but didn't seem to think there was much they could do.

'Can't you arrest him?' I pleaded.

They couldn't. Not on the basis of a phone call, a single allegation, even such a serious one.

I explained about the divorce, the beatings – the court order to get him out of the house. 'I'm scared he'll break in and torch the place,' I said, desperate. 'There must be *something* you can do.'

The officer asked me wait. I put my hand on my chest and felt my heart thudding. I ran to the back door, checked the bolts were in, and yanked the kitchen curtains shut. All of a sudden the house didn't feel nearly as secure as I'd thought it was. I picked up the phone again and waited for the policeman to come back on the line.

Uniformed officers would keep an eye out later, he said. It was the best he could do. 'If you hear any more from your husband in the meantime, get straight back on to us.'

In the quiet of the night as the house settled down I heard creaks and groans I'd never noticed before. The smallest of sounds had me jumping up to check on the children. Every time a car went past I ran to the window to see if it was Nick.

At midnight a police patrol car cruised down the street and parked under the street lamp opposite. Every few minutes, I checked to make sure it was still there. At first light, I drew back the bedroom curtains. The street was quiet, just a milk float slowly making its way down. The police car hadn't moved. I went downstairs and put the knife back in the kitchen drawer.

30.

The stress of the divorce had taken a toll on my skin. I had terrible eczema and acne. My face was inflamed and blotchy, covered in painful lumps and bumps. It throbbed and itched and drove me to distraction. I picked at it and scratched until it was badly scarred and pocked with craters.

I became so self-conscious I took to keeping my head down when I was out in the hope no one would notice me. It wasn't just my face. My hands were raw and cracked from the eczema. In shops, I could see assistants flinching in disgust when I handed over money.

I went to my GP and tried to tell him how bad I was feeling but got the impression he didn't see problem skin as something serious. 'You've got a bit of acne,' he said, as if I was making a fuss about nothing. A bit of acne! 'These things tend to come and go.' He gave me a prescription for some kind of medicated cream. 'My advice is to try not to get so worked up,' he said.

I knew what he was thinking; that it was vanity on my part.

There was much more to it than that. I had no confidence. I could barely look people in the eye. The constant itching meant I wasn't even sleeping well. When the cream he gave me made no difference I went back and was given another prescription.

It seemed to make my skin worse than ever.

If I thought Nick would lose interest and leave us alone I was wrong. A few months after threatening to burn the house down he was back in touch, saying he hadn't meant any of it. It was just him lashing out in frustration.

'Don't forget, it wasn't me wanted any of this,' he said. 'I still care about you, whatever you think.' He had a funny way of showing it. 'I want to come round, see the kids. No funny business, I swear.'

Despite what had gone on between us I had no desire to stop him having a relationship with his children. Michele was eleven and Michael nearly four. I didn't want them growing up not knowing their father. A couple of nights later, Nick turned up. Late. The children had been at the window looking out for him, getting excited, then disappointed, every time a car went past. Memories of being stood up as a teenager tied my stomach in knots. I was about to send them to bed when he finally appeared, suited and booted, ready for a night out by the look of things. The kids jumped on him, delighted.

'Mind me suit, will you. Watch where you're putting them sticky fingers,' he said, as they pawed at him.

Same old Nick.

'You were supposed to be here more than an hour ago,' I said.

'I had to change a tyre.'

For someone who worked in the motor trade, I had never known anyone have so much car trouble.

He smoothed down his suit where Michael had been hanging onto him. 'So, where do you fancy going?' he asked me.

'I'm not going anywhere,' I said.

'We could go for a drink, a drive out …'

'Have you seen the time?' The children were looking from him to me, not sure what was happening. 'They should be in bed,' I said.

He shrugged. 'We can get a babysitter.'

We. Unbelievable. I showed him the door. 'If you arrange to be here at a certain time, stick to it,' I said. 'They've been at the window keeping lookout half the night.'

'Next time we'll go out,' he promised.

The following week he turned up when he was supposed to. 'Get ready, we're going out,' he told me.

'I thought you were taking the kids.'

'I said I would, didn't I? Soon as you're ready we'll go.'

'Not me. The kids.'

'What, you're not coming?'

I shook my head.

'I've come all this way and now you tell me,' he said, rattled.

'You were only ever coming to see the kids.'

He gave me a long hard look. 'What's wrong with your face?' I looked away, embarrassed. He came closer, peered at me. 'God you're looking really ugly these days, Jenny,' he said.

With that, he turned and went.

31.

My skin was in a shocking state.

I got into the habit of wearing thick layers of make-up and spent ages each morning filling in the craters that littered my face, carefully blending foundation with concealer, only for it to dry out and fall off in lumps as the day wore on. It was humiliating. I'd be sitting on a train and see the person opposite looking at me oddly, then I'd spot a chunk of make-up in my lap. I wasn't getting anywhere with my GP so I made an appointment with a dermatologist, a professor, in Harley Street. If I saw an expert, surely I'd get the help I needed.

The professor's clinic was on the ground floor of a grand-looking house with a glossy black front door and a brass nameplate. The waiting room had plush mismatched sofas, a fish tank; a receptionist in a white coat. The professor, grey hair slicked back, horn-rimmed specs, sat behind a desk in a consulting room with a fireplace and huge sash windows. There were travel posters on the wall. Berlin. Paris. Rome. Places I hadn't been to.

I told him about the eczema and the spots and the non-stop itching. He peered at me across the desk. 'You've got a bit of acne,' he said, echoing my GP. 'It's almost impossible to know the cause.'

I tried to say I thought stress was at the root of it.

He shook his head. 'There's a lot of nonsense talked about stress, if you ask me,' he said.

Before I knew it I was heading home with a prescription for something I'd had before. I couldn't help thinking I'd just parted with my hard-earned cash for nothing. As time wore on I must have seen at least a dozen so-called specialists. Every time I came across a story in a newspaper or magazine about problem skin I followed up on whoever they quoted and went to see them. They were all happy to take my money yet not a single one managed to help me.

In the end, I decided to sort it out myself.

I spent hours in the library poring over medical reference books, finding out how the skin worked. I learned that cells were constantly renewing themselves and it was possible to speed things up using peeling agents. I experimented on my own damaged skin using alpha hydroxy acids, bit by bit stripping away the scarred surface layer, revealing fresh, clear skin underneath. It was a slow and tortuous process, trial and error. I was working with chemicals, not knowing what strength to use or how long to leave them on. Sometimes I got it wrong and the pain was excruciating but I persevered, learning the whole time, refining my methods. I never felt like giving up. I was on a mission to have porcelain skin and had every confidence I could do it. In all the reading I was doing it seemed Canada was leading the way when it came to treating skin problems. I kept coming across the same names – doctors with a reputation for getting results – and I got in touch to pick their brains. They confirmed I was on the right track.

After fourteen months, my skin was flawless.

I was still nursing at night and working as many days as I could in the salon and needed help at home so I got a demi-pair – basically, a live-in nanny who looked after the children in return for board and lodging. Demi-pairs were mostly young girls who wanted to be in London for whatever reason. The first one who came to stay was April, from Devon. She seemed easy going and eager to please. She had hardly been with us a week when I came home from work one morning and heard her shouting down the stairs to the children for a cup of tea. 'And not so much milk this time,' she boomed. 'When I was your age I was doing breakfast in bed for my parents.'

I ran upstairs and flung open the door to her room. She was sprawled in bed, radio on, flicking through a magazine. Her face dropped. 'Out!' I said. 'Right now.'

Next was Yolanda from Austria. She was a nice smiley girl. The children liked her, and we got along. She had been with us a few weeks when Michael came downstairs one day with a necklace I'd been searching high and low for.

'Where did you find that? I said.

'Yolanda had it,' he said.

'Show me.'

Under her bed was a suitcase of mine stuffed with my belongings: books, fashion jewellery, ornaments, some Yardley soaps, an evening bag, a scarf, a sparkly top I'd turned the place upside down looking for, a suede jacket ... I couldn't understand why she was squirrelling away my clothes since I let her borrow anything she wanted anyway. When I showed her what I'd found she shrugged and said Michael must have put them there.

After Yolanda, Toshi arrived. She was from Japan and was the sweetest little thing. The children adored her. She was with us for several months. There were two or three more, some good, some not so good. I had to take my chances and hope for the best. Without them, I couldn't have managed. Every so often, Nick came round, supposedly to see the children, and each time we had the same performance – him twisting my arm to go out with him, me refusing. The kids barely got a look-in. It incensed me. I took to letting him in and disappearing to the bathroom where I'd sit on the loo knitting, in the hope he would take the hint and spend time with Michele and Michael. Instead, he followed me upstairs and knocked on the door, pleading with me to come out and talk to him. We weren't getting anywhere.

'You can't keep doing this,' I said. 'They get all excited wanting to see you, then you show up and ignore them. It's not fair.'

'I'll make it up to them,' he said. 'Take them for a pizza next time.'

A few days later when he arrived the kids were ready to go out. Nick took one look at me and his face fell. 'You're not even ready,' he said,' settling himself in an armchair. Michael tried to climb on his lap. Nick pushed him back down. 'You know we're going out,' he said, giving me an accusing look.

Not this again. 'You said you'd take the kids for pizza,' I reminded him.

'You always do this,' he said, getting annoyed. 'What is your problem?'

The kids looked anxious. 'They've been looking forward to seeing you,' I said, doing my best to keep things light. 'Tell you what, why don't you take them to the place on the high street?'

Nick was shaking his head. 'Just get ready will you?'

The way he said it, belligerent and bossy, put my back up. The days of him ordering me about were over. 'I've told you, I'm not coming,' I said.

He got to his feet. 'Suit yourself. No one's going, in that case.'

I took the kids out for pizza myself. Gradually, the visits from their father dried up.

32.

July 7, 1983. 1.30 a.m.

'All is quiet as the wing sleeps so I thought I would write to say it was good to meet my new friend, Jenny. I have been thinking of you. Wish you could share those thoughts!!! It was real good because it will be a long time before I can get physical...'

I knew who had written the letter before I opened it. 'H.M. Prison Parkhurst' on the front of the envelope gave it away. It was from the gangster, Reg Kray. The messy scrawl covered four pages, the words tumbling down each sheet as if they were sliding down a slope into a gulley at the bottom right hand corner. It took me a while to get to grips with the handwriting. 'You know the eyes are the-' I couldn't make out the next word – *something* – 'of the soul.' The *window*? No. The *opening*? It turned out to be *outlet*. Reg had his own style, alright. 'When I looked into your eyes they told me a little tale that one day I'll relate to you,' he wrote.

I pictured him in his cell propped up on an elbow in bed in the early hours, radio on low, scribbling away by torchlight. It probably wasn't anything like that. I'd heard about 'lights out' and assumed prisoners were plunged into darkness at a set time every night but had no idea what really went on in a high security jail. As far as I knew, he could keep the light on all night if he felt like it. Maybe he had a proper little table in the corner of the room where he wrote his letters. Day to day life in prison was a complete mystery to me. I had never mixed with villains and certainly didn't plan on getting to know one of the most notorious criminals of the twentieth century. Reg signed off the letter with, 'Sleep well. God bless. Lots of love, your new friend Scorpio xxx.'

It was official. I was Reggie Kray's new friend.

And it was all down to my sister, Lizzie.

When I was growing up, Lizzie was always immaculate. If she was going out she'd have her hair done, the short brown style tinted red at the front. Doing her make-up took hours and she'd check it in every possible light. She was slim, proud of her flat stomach, and her clothes were just-so. There were seventeen years between us and when I was little Lizzie was out having a good time in London. It was the sixties and she was mixing in the same circles as the Kray twins, rubbing shoulders with Reg and Ron, who pretty much ran east London then.

Once the twins were sent down for murder, in 1969, Lizzie was no longer in touch and it stayed that way until their mum, Violet, died, in August, 1982. The funeral just about brought the East End to a standstill. Reg and Ron were allowed out of prison to attend, handcuffed and flanked by warders. The news footage prompted Lizzie to write to Reg to say how sorry she was he'd lost his mum. He wrote back and that was the start of her visiting him in Parkhurst. Lizzie was in love with Reggie, not that I knew anything about it. I'm not sure Reggie did either. I only found out when she turned up on my doorstep in Newbury Park one day and announced she had left her husband and was moving in with me. Before I had a chance to object she was making herself at home in the spare room.

Lizzie had always been forceful, a bit on the bossy side. When I was little I'd be cheeky to her and wind her up until she was ready to throttle me. I was good at avoiding a hiding though, small enough to squeeze under a piece of furniture and lie low. It didn't pay to let Lizzie catch up with you. She could be a bit slap happy.

Once she moved in with me all I heard was Reg Kray this and Reg Kray that. She was besotted. Of course, she told him she had left home and was living with her divorced little sister and, next thing, Reg had arranged two visiting orders and told Lizzie to bring me to Parkhurst.

'I'm not going,' I told her, when she broached the subject.

'Why not? He's a nice bloke,' Lizzie said.

'He's inside for murder!'

'He wants to meet you and you don't say no to Reg Kray.'

'*I* do.' I was indignant. 'No way am I going to Parkhurst. You'd better tell him.'

Lizzie wrote and broke the news. Another letter arrived from Reg. 'If your sister won't come you needn't bother either,' he wrote.

She was furious. 'See what you've done, you selfish little cow. It's not as if I ever ask you to do anything for me.'

That wasn't strictly true. She had asked to move in with me, hadn't she? Come to think of it, it hadn't exactly been a request – more a case of her showing up and me making up the spare bed.

She glared at me. 'One visit, that's all you have to do and you won't. Oh no, won't put yourself out for me, will you, little cow.'

A memory flooded back from when I was about seven years old and my sister Christine borrowed one of Lizzie's coats without asking. It was a good one: camel, double-breasted, big shiny buttons. With her black hair and hazel eyes Christine was a looker. To me, she was like the film star Elizabeth Taylor. She was also the opposite of Lizzie and never made much of an effort with her appearance. Christine was the type to have a fag hanging from the corner of her mouth and tuck her hair under a turban rather than have it done. She was the sort to sling her coat over the back of a chair and not notice when it fell on the floor. The day Lizzie found out that Christine had flounced off up the West End in her best coat she was livid. She stomped into the kitchen and all you could hear was a drawer being yanked open and cutlery clattering about. When she came back into the living room she had a carving knife in her hand. Her plan was to wait for Christine to come home and give her what-for. Time wore on and Lizzie went to bed, still clutching the knife. Luckily, she fell asleep and by the morning with the coat safely back in the wardrobe on its hanger she had calmed down. Remembering that episode, I couldn't help thinking maybe she and Reg were well-suited. At the same time I didn't want to end up on the wrong side of her.

'Alright,' I said, 'I'll go. Just this once.' I was determined that would be it. One visit to keep the peace with Lizzie, nothing more.

What I hadn't reckoned on was that I'd actually get along with Reg Kray and we'd end up writing to each other. Never in a million years did I think that visit would be the first of many I'd make to Parkhurst over the coming year.

Lizzie and I got the train from Waterloo to Portsmouth. I was nervous and she seemed to be too because she kept disappearing to the loo. It was only when we were on the south coast and boarding the ferry to the Isle of Wight that I noticed something slightly odd about her. She was … well, a bit tipsy. She must have had a bottle of something in her bag and all those trips to the loo were cover for a sneaky swig.

When we got to the prison all I could see was a high wall topped with some kind of wire. Although it was a Category A jail, getting in was a lot more straightforward than I'd expected it to be. A warder went through my bag and then we were ushered into the grounds and up a metal staircase that led to the visitors' room. It was all very informal, a big cafeteria-style place with chairs and tables and a hatch in one of the walls where you could get tea and snacks.

Lizzie and I sat at a table and waited for Reg to arrive. I'd seen plenty of pictures in the papers and on the TV news and as soon as he walked in, slim and muscular in a blue tee-shirt and casual trousers, I recognised him. Lizzie's face lit up. Reg had a young lad in his twenties in tow. His name was Steve Tully and he was introduced to us as Reg's 'adopted son.'

Reg was supposed to sit opposite Lizzie but he took the chair facing me. Steve Tully settled into the spare seat across from Lizzie. I didn't dare catch her eye. Reg sat forward, arms folded on the table, looking hard at me. His gaze was intense. My mouth felt dry. I didn't like the way he was staring. It made me think of a mad dog. There was a faint smile on his lips. I felt peculiar, as if I couldn't get my breath, and my heart was beating fast. He leaned across the table and said, 'Don't be shy.' He was so softly spoken I had to lean in to hear him. Our noses were almost touching. His short greying hair was combed back. A few wispy hairs sprouted from his ears. The back of my neck felt damp.

'You're very attractive,' he said. 'Tell me about yourself.'

Next to Reg, Steve was making small talk with Lizzie, asking about the crossing from Portsmouth. I felt a knot of fear in my stomach. She hadn't come all this way dolled up to the nines and smelling of Opium to talk about the Isle of Wight ferry. Only a few seconds into the visit and already it was going horribly wrong. Without even glancing in her direction, I knew she was giving me filthy looks.

'I wish I'd known you when I was on the outside,' Reg said.

I couldn't help laughing. He and Ron had been sentenced at the Old Bailey to a minimum of thirty years in 1969. 'Reg, I was practically in primary school when you were on the outside,' I said.

That made him laugh. 'I like your smile, Jenny.' Suddenly,

his expression turned serious. 'Now, I want you to do something for me.' I felt my smile collapse. 'No need to look so worried now. I want you to promise you'll send me a photo.'

A photo. Was that all? I nodded, relieved.

He reached across the table and touched my hand. A scar was visible on the inside of his wrist. 'You promise?'

'All right, I'll send a picture.'

Lizzie was going to kill me.

He talked about having a party, him and his brother Ron, who was in Broadmoor, when they were finally released. 'I want a slow dance with you, Jenny,' he said. 'I'm booking it now.'

At the end of visiting time, I got up to go and Reg stepped to the side of the table, got hold of me, tipped me backwards and planted a big kiss on my lips. It was the second time in the space of an hour I'd not been able to get my breath.

Lizzie really was going to kill me.

On the way home she and I sat on the train in silence, her mouth set in a hard angry line. She didn't say a word.

A couple of days later I was in the garden repairing the broken wall at the front of the house when she finally rounded on me.

'If this is how you treat your sister I'd hate to be your friend,' she said, loud enough for the neighbours to hear. 'I saw you, all over him. You couldn't take your eyes off him!'

'I didn't dare, you mean.'

'You're a little cow!'

'Lizzie, what on earth would I want with him? He's too old,

for one thing.'

I thought she was going to pick up one of the bricks lying on the ground and hit me with it. I took a step back. 'In any case,' I said, 'he's a criminal.'

She gave me a look of disgust. As far as she was concerned I had stolen her beloved Reggie. It was weeks before we were on speaking terms again.

33.

What surprised me most about Reg Kray was that I got to like him. It might sound strange but he struck me as a decent bloke. I couldn't help thinking there were a lot worse than him who spent less time inside.

By the time I met him he'd had a breakdown and tried to kill himself on more than one occasion. I could certainly relate to that. What separated us was that he had blood on his hands. Then again, for a long time I felt I did too. Plenty of people, me included, reckoned I had killed my parents. The year 1969 had been a turning point, both for me and for Reggie. I'd lost my parents and he had lost his liberty and was starting his sentence with its minimum thirty-year recommendation. Despite the age difference between us we seemed to understand each other. After that first visit with Lizzie, I made the trip to the Isle of Wight to see him every few weeks.

Even though I was making regular visits, he sent me letters and I wrote back. I went into Parkhurst one day and he had a gift for me, a clock he'd made in the prison workshop. On another occasion he presented me with a caravan made out of matchsticks. I've still got both gifts. I'd take him stuff as well. Once, he asked if I could get a sheepskin rug for his cell. I didn't want to say I hadn't the money for it but at home I did have a little black sheepskin that I rolled up and took in next time I went to see him. He was so pleased with it. It was good for me talking to Reg; he was always a good listener, interested in what I was doing.

We had more in common than I would ever have thought possible.

Reg put me in touch with a girl he knew, Elaine Mildener, and we'd visit the prison together. Elaine was striking-looking with a fondness for sharp tailoring and shoulder pads. The bigger, the better. One day, the pair of us were sitting with Reg when she took herself off to the toilet, strutting across the visitors' room, oozing attitude in her heels. I couldn't help smiling. Reg gave me a nudge. 'Gangster's moll,' he said, chuckling.

Elaine told me that when she was a schoolgirl living on the Peabody Estate in Islington a big black car cruised down the road one day, pulled up, and out got the Kray twins. She turned to her friend, impressed. 'One day I'm going to marry one of them,' she said.

All the time I was friendly with Reg, I was seeing a guy called Billy. It was nothing serious but he was a lovely bloke, a good laugh, always paying me compliments, which was what I needed after what had gone on with my marriage. It turned out he knew the Krays too. As a young lad, Billy was into boxing and went down the gym in Bethnal Green where he met Ronnie, who took a shine to him and started coaching him. One night they were somewhere and couldn't get home because the weather was bad and Billy ended up sharing a bed with Ronnie. Propped up in the corner of the room was a sawn-off shotgun. Before long, Billy felt a big hairy arm slide over him and jumped out of bed. He stood with his hands covering his bits, scared half to death.

'Not me, Ron! I'm not like that, Ron!'

'It's either that,' Ron said, pointing at Billy's shaking hands. 'Or' – he turned to the shotgun in the corner – 'it's that.'

Billy shook his head. 'Sorry, Ron, you're going to have to shoot me!'

Ron just laughed. 'Get back into bed, son, you're alright.'

The rest of the night passed without incident.

I went to a few glamorous parties with Billy, some of them full of villains. At one, a charity event to do with the Krays where the star turn was Cyndi Lauper, I had my picture taken with the twins' elder brother, Charlie.

Much as I enjoyed seeing Reg, I had the feeling I was being drawn into something I wasn't entirely comfortable with. During one visit, he told me Ron wanted me to go and see him in Broadmoor.

'I've told him all about you,' he said. 'He can't wait to meet you.'

No way was I going to Broadmoor.

What finally put an end to things was Steve Tully coming out of prison, constantly phoning in the middle of the night, wanting to send a car to pick me up so we could go clubbing.

It was one thing visiting Reg inside, another having his 'son' pester me on the outside.

I let Reg know I wouldn't be visiting any more.

A couple of years later, in 1985, just as she predicted, Elaine married Ron in Broadmoor. The moll had got her gangster.

34.

It was never my plan to open a skin care clinic. I carried on nursing at night and working at the salon as many days as I could manage, doing nails, until a lorry ran into the back of me at a red light in Ilford. The car was a mess but I didn't think I was hurt until I woke up in agony the next day. I had whiplash, so debilitating I was no longer able to do any lifting. That was the end of my nursing career. From then on, I worked flat out at the salon, learning everything I could about the beauty business. A lot of people who'd seen my skin at its worst wondered how I'd managed to get it looking so good and wanted me to do the same for them so I started doing facials at home, experimenting with products, getting great results. What was interesting was how much better people seemed to feel about everything once their skin was clear and healthy-looking. As well as doing wonders for their confidence, good skin seemed to make them an awful lot happier as well. It was a joy for me seeing clients blossom. By the early nineties I was in demand, working non-stop, and at the same time going through the horrors of the teenage years with Michael. I would look at my lovely, loving son and wonder what on earth had happened to turn him into a sullen, grunting, irritable stranger.

'What have you done with Michael?' I'd say, as he slobbed about the place, scowling, barely speaking.

By now, Michele was twenty-something and all grown up. I remembered going through the same thing with her when she was in her teens. With both my children it seemed as if once they reached adolescence they became alien beings. I really wished someone had warned me that, in time, things get back to normal. The teenage Michael wanted nothing to do with me. I missed him! Luckily, the young lad who lived a couple of doors down from us always had a smile and a kind word when I saw him. Invariably, however bad I was feeling, he managed to cheer me up. Funny how things work out. A few years later, that same young lad – Paul – married my daughter.

With my beauty business taking off, I set up the Dynasty Clinic in the Great Eastern Hotel next to Liverpool Street Station in London. It was a good spot but I'd only been there a year or so when Terence Conran bought the place and I had to get out. A lot of businesses were in the same boat and the Corporation of London stepped in and offered all of us new premises nearby at 65 London Wall.

I knew from my own experience it was possible to transform even the worst skin. A lot of the women I saw had already sought help from countless so-called experts and got nowhere, just as I once had. Some arrived thoroughly sceptical, convinced no one could help them – although not for long. My attitude was that something could always be done and my mission was to make everyone who came to see me feel better about themselves. Only once was I unable to help a client, a woman who had terrible gouges and wheals on her face. I had never seen anything like it and nothing I did was helping. Every time she came in, her skin was the same, if not worse. Eventually, she admitted she was self-harming.

Some of my clients, having lived with awful acne for years, found it not only cleared up but their skin looked years younger in the process. I started making my own products, playing with ingredients, chopping and changing things around, until I developed a range that did what I needed. At night I lay awake thinking about what would happen if I combined such-and-such with so-and-so and in the early hours scribbled down ideas on a notepad at the side of the bed. My kitchen became more a makeshift lab for blending skincare concoctions than a place for cooking. When a friend was suffering from awful eczema I played with different formulas until I came up with something that cleared it up. I called it Pink Heaven and in no time it had become my star product.

I never stopped learning, soaking up every bit of knowledge I could. When I heard about Danné Montague-King, a scientist in California with a reputation for being streets ahead of everyone else when it came to skin, I scrimped and saved, sold every bit of jewellery I owned, and went to train with him. Mainly through word of mouth, people heard about the work I was doing and things snowballed. Women, and men, from all walks of life – from politicians and peers of the realm to pop stars – now come to see me.

When I moved into the London Wall premises they were supposed to be a stopping off place until I found somewhere more permanent. Little did I know I would get so busy, so fast, there would be no time to think about another move and, almost twenty years on, I'm still in my 'temporary' home …

35.

In 2012, I was due to have a routine mammogram but couldn't make the appointment. While I was waiting for it to be rearranged I noticed some tenderness in one of my breasts. I wasn't in any pain but thought I should have it looked at and got onto the screening people to see about speeding up my appointment. They referred me back to my GP. Weeks went by and I couldn't get in to see him. In the meantime, what had started as a smallish area of tender tissue had developed into a painful swelling. I was thinking it must be some kind of infection and that I was probably going to need a course of antibiotics to clear it up. While I was still waiting to see my doctor I bumped into my friend, Carol, a radiographer at a clinic in the same building as me, and asked what she thought I should do. She offered to do a mammogram there and then.

Although she did her best to give nothing away, from the look on her face I guessed something was wrong.

Less than a week later, on September 6, I was called to the one-stop breast diagnostic clinic at London Bridge Hospital to see the specialist there, Nicolas Beechey-Newman. Carol came with me but I was fine on my own and once we got to the clinic I sent her away.

'Don't think the worst,' Mr Beechey-Newman said, following an initial examination. 'I'm certainly not. If it does turn out to be bad news, we'll deal with it.'

I had blood tests, another mammogram, a scan, a biopsy. They all but turned me upside down and rattled me. Three hours later, I was back in the consultant's office, this time with the oncology nurse present. I thought, 'This doesn't look good.'

'I hate to tell you this but you have breast cancer,' Mr Beechey-Newman said. He seemed so upset I was afraid he might cry.

'Come on, now,' I said, 'there's no need to look like that, is there? We'll work it out. What's the plan?'

He glanced at the oncology nurse. 'The tests show you have breast cancer,' he repeated, perhaps thinking from my reaction that I hadn't understood what he had just told me.

'Well, it can't be all that bad,' I went on. 'Tell me what happens next and I'll help you.'

I was going to need more tests, he said, and then they would decide how best to treat me.

I asked if someone could get me a taxi back to Liverpool Street and the nurse offered to flag one down for me. Outside, on Tooley Street, as we looked for a black cab with a light on, she went over on her ankle, twisting it badly. Just then a cab swung into the kerb and she bundled me in. I watched, concerned, as she hobbled back down the street to the hospital entrance. All night, she was on my mind. I had visions of her with her leg in plaster. Next morning, first thing, she phoned to see how I was feeling.

'I know it's a shock, a lot to get your head round,' she said. 'It can take a while for news like that to sink in.'

'Never mind about that,' I said. 'How's your ankle?'

I heard what sounded like a sharp intake of breath on the other end of the line. 'My *ankle*?' she said.

'It's not broken, is it?'

'No, it's not broken, it's …' she seemed a bit thrown.

'Well, *that's* good news, isn't it?' I said.

'Well, yes, it's … Jenny, we've just given you news you've got breast cancer and you're asking how my *ankle* is.'

'Oh, I know about *that*. We can deal with *that*. As long as you're alright …'

I wasn't feeling quite as casual about the diagnosis as it may have appeared. My biggest worry was how I was going to break the news to my children. I was hoping all I'd need was a smallish operation, a lumpectomy, and that I could nip in and out of hospital without having to tell anyone what was going on.

At my next appointment with Mr Beechey-Newman another scan confirmed there were three separate tumours, all in the same breast.

'I'm so sorry, I'm afraid it's going to have to be a mastectomy,' he said.

He explained they would be able to do a breast reconstruction at the same time as the mastectomy. It was a major procedure, he said, and I would be in hospital for at least five days. So much for nipping in and out and keeping quiet about it.

'Well, that's alright, whatever we've got to do,' I said, trying to hide my disappointment.

'I really am very sorry,' he said. 'I know it's not the news you wanted.'

'Don't keep saying sorry,' I told him. 'Look on the bright side – what girl doesn't want a boob job?'

He shook his head, smiling. 'You really are a breath of fresh air. I do so enjoy you coming to see me.'

I laughed. 'I only wish I could say the same.'

That night, my son-in-law, Paul, phoned and I decided to confide in him. 'Do you remember me saying that if ever I needed help I could talk to you and it wouldn't go any further?'

'Course I do. What's wrong?' he said.

'I can't actually say it, you're going to have to guess,' I said.

'Right ... are you ill?'

I said about going for tests and needing treatment, not quite managing to tell him what the actual problem was.

Paul didn't say anything straight away. Eventually, he said, 'Have you got what Mum had?' Three years before, his mum had died from ovarian cancer.

I said it was breast cancer and that I needed surgery. 'I don't want the children to know,' I said.

The next morning he phoned. 'No way will you get away without telling them,' he said. 'Apart from anything, if Michele found out you'd been through something like this without a word I don't think she'd ever forgive you.'

He had a point. 'So, how you going to tell her, then?' I asked.

'I'll break the news softly, softly.'

That night, before he had a chance to broach the subject, Michele started on about how she was worried because she kept phoning me at work and I seemed to be away from the clinic a lot, having mystery appointments.

'No one knows where she is,' Michele said. 'I'm sure something's wrong. In fact, I think she's found a lump in her breast and she's not telling anyone. It would be just like her.'

'Actually, she has,' Paul said.

Michele was staggered. 'What, you know more than me? Has she got an appointment with a specialist?'

'It's a bit more than that.'

'What, she's having tests?'

'Bit more than that. She's got breast cancer and she's got to have a mastectomy.'

Michele dissolved in tears but not for long. In no time she had rallied and was making plans.

'We need to work out how we're going to deal with this,' she told me, making it clear there would be no more sneaking off to the hospital without her.

From then on, she took over and was with me at every turn – determined, upbeat and full of fighting spirit; a real tonic.

One thing I noticed was that once you're diagnosed with cancer the phone never stops ringing. Lots of the calls were from specialist nurses who had a tendency to talk in soft, whispered tones. They were keen to arrange counselling, which was kind of them, but talking to a stranger about my cancer wasn't for me. I preferred to focus on the practicalities of the treatment rather than dwell too much on the whys and wherefores of having the disease. I won't pretend I didn't have my moments when I thought about dying. Cancer tends to make you feel like that. Mostly, though, I just wanted to get on with dealing with it and do everything in my power to defeat it.

On September 29, a little over three weeks after being diagnosed, I went in for my operation. Michele had made arrangements to have a spare bed in my room so that she could be with me throughout my stay. I honestly think the only time she let me out of her sight was when they took me into theatre and if she could have done she'd have come with me then, too.

It took five hours to remove the breast and do the reconstruction using pig skin, a relatively new method that meant my plastic surgeon, Mr Mark Ho Asjoe, didn't have to take skin from my back and was able to keep scarring to a minimum. When I started to come round after the surgery, Michele was there at my bedside. It took a while for the anaesthetic to wear off and until it did she didn't get much sense out of me. All I kept saying was, 'Is it over?'

As soon as I was properly conscious I wanted to see what they'd done. I know for many women a mastectomy conjures up brutal and disfiguring surgery but all I can say is that in my case the surgeons did the most amazing work and I was delighted with the result. After a few months, I went back in and they matched up the other breast. Again, Michele, stuck like glue, and slept in my room.

Once the surgical procedures were completed the next

thing was to work out follow-up treatment. Now that I had breast implants, radiotherapy wasn't an option and, since chemotherapy only benefitted something like three patients out of every 100, it was hardly worth considering. Because my tumours were fed by the hormone oestrogen the main thing was to stop the body from producing any more and the best way of doing that was a five year course of the drug, Tamoxifen. It has taken some getting used to. As I write this, more than two years on, I still have moments when I struggle with severe side effects: bouts of nausea, morning sickness, nails dropping off, my hair coming out in clumps. When I mentioned this to Mr Beechey-Newman he said there were other drugs they could look at that might help with the hair and nail loss but because I suffered from arthritis the likely side-effects would be pain in my joints.

I decided to stick with Tamoxifen.

In 2013, about a year or so after I'd had the mastectomy I started getting cystitis and was always at the doctor being prescribed different antibiotics. Nothing got rid of it and eventually I was in such desperate pain I had a scan that showed a cyst on the ovary. In January, 2014, I was back at the London Bridge Hospital seeing a gynaecologist, Mr Andrea Papadopoulos. It's funny how names can conjure up images. For some reason, I'd convinced myself Mr Papadopoulos was an older gentleman, short and swarthy, on the podgy side, with thinning black hair. When the door to his consulting room opened and my gynaecologist turned out to be a dead ringer for George Clooney I almost fell off my chair. More examinations, scans and blood tests followed. It turned out I needed more surgery to remove the cyst and fallopian tubes.

'If there's any cancer present the chances of it having spread to the uterus are very small so we won't need to do a hysterectomy,' George – I mean, Mr Papadopoulos – said

I looked at him. 'Whenever anyone talks about a *small chance* of something happening that usually means me.'

'We'll do a biopsy of the uterus, just to be sure,' he said.

Sure enough, the biopsy found cancerous cells in the fallopian tubes as well as the uterus. Two months later, in March 2014, I was back in theatre having the cervix, uterus and the omentum – the apron of skin that hangs down in front of the intestines – removed. On each of the four occasions I went into hospital Michele was with me, sleeping in my room. Not for a moment was I left on my own. She was amazing, my angel child. Michael was just as good, a rock, supporting me at every turn. I couldn't help thinking our roles had reversed and remembered him as a youngster having a hard time at school, me going to get him and make a bacon sandwich to cheer him up. Now, it was his turn.

'If you want to come home, any time, day or night, just let me know and I'll come and get you,' he said. '*And* do you a bacon sandwich.'

So far, I'm doing well, although at the time of writing, in June 2015, I have yet to be given the all-clear.

More than anything, having cancer has made me realise just how precious time is. Every day is a bonus. Being around the people I care about, having good experiences – those are the things that mean the most. I'm more aware than ever before that life is short and unpredictable; that nothing can be taken for granted. Not many of us want to talk about death, or even think about it, yet it's something we all have to face – often when we least expect it. I've come to terms with that and, without being morbid, I'm not afraid of dying.

It's how I live my life that counts.

Writing this book has meant shining a light on some of the darkest corners of my past, going back to places filled with painful memories. Getting it down on paper has been a lot more difficult than I imagined, almost like going through a gruelling form of therapy at times.

For years I was the selfish little cow who killed my parents. Guilt and grief very nearly dragged me under. I got it into my head I was a bad person and deserved to suffer. No wonder I ended up in an abusive marriage and stayed there so long. Now, the only men I trust are my son, my son-in-law and my grandson.

I now know that when you're vulnerable it's easy to mistake controlling and manipulative behaviour for love. I don't blame myself for that, just as I no longer blame myself for the deaths of my parents, although in both cases it took a long while to see the light.

Remembering my younger self it's as if I'm talking about someone else, not me. The older Jenny wouldn't have put up with the half of it. At the same time, I've come to understand that all I went through – the bad as well as the good – has made me who I am today.

I genuinely believe it's possible to turn things around, no matter what. I'm living proof. Through sheer hard work and a passion for what I do I've created the life I once dreamed of … the house, the swimming pool, the car on the drive. More important, I have the peace of mind that comes from a sense of being fulfilled and complete.

When I think about the past, I don't waste time regretting the things I did or didn't do, or wish my life had taken a different turn. I'm too busy thinking about the here and now, making the most of each precious moment.

Happy in my own skin, at last.

About the Author

Jenny Harding set up the Dynasty Clinic, in London, in the 1990s. Since then, her reputation as a skincare guru has spread far and wide and she draws clients from all over the world.

Find out more about Jenny at **www.dynastyclinic.net**
Follow Jenny on twitter **@DynastyClinic**

Acknowledgments

Without Maria Malone this book would never have been written. It was only because she kept on at me and never gave up that it happened.

She is a true friend as well as a brilliant author.
www.mariamalonebooks.com